# Public Policies for an Aging Population

# The Boston University Series in Gerontology

## Boston University Gerontology Center

The Gerontology Center is a multidisciplinary organization that integrates the biological, psychological, socioeconomic, medical and humanistic concerns of aging and of the elderly.

# Public Policies for an Aging Population

Edited by

**Elizabeth W. Markson**
**Gretchen R. Batra**

The Gerontology Center
of Boston University

**LexingtonBooks**

D.C. Heath and Company
Lexington, Massachusetts
Toronto

**Library of Congress Cataloging in Publication Data**

Main entry under title:

Public policies for an aging population.

(Boston University series in gerontology)
"Evolved from the Boston University Summer Institute in Gerontology, sponsored by the Boston University Gerontology Center and Summer Term."
1. Aged policy—United States—Congresses. I. Markson, Elizabeth Warren. II. Batra, Gretchen. III. Boston University. Summer Institute in Gerontology. IV. Series: Boston University. Boston University series in gerontology.
HQ1064.U5P76                    362.6'0973                    79-3249
ISBN 0-669-03398-7

Published simultaneously in Canada

Printed in the United States of America

International Standard Book Number: 0-669-03398-7

Library of Congress Catalog Card Number: 79-3249

# Contents

# Preface and Acknowledgments

This collection of essays evolved from the Boston University Summer Institute in Gerontology, sponsored by the Boston University Gerontology Center and Summer Term. This first volume in the Boston University Series in Gerontology focuses on selected policy issues in social gerontology. Three questions stimulated our thinking and guided selection of the topics: What are the most salient issues requiring action at the policy level if we are to develop rational and humane social programs geared to the one in nine Americans who are sixty-five and over at the present time? What common threads run through our currently tangled skeins of educational, social, and health services for the aged? How may these be woven into a more cohesive social fabric for the elderly of future generations? While much has been said in recent years about quality of life in old age, this quality, like the weather, remains more talked about than purposefully planned or altered.

Too often, policy analyses suffer either from global approaches of the motherhood-and-apple-pie variety or from the overspecificity dictated by a particular discipline. In soliciting original essays for this book, we looked for and chose authors who would bring not only the perspective of their disciplines but also a broader concern with directions for national policies regarding older adults and diversity of opinion. The contributors to this book include scholars from the fields of anthropology, education, philosophy, political economics, social work, and sociology, and they have all been associated with the Boston University Summer Institute in Gerontology.

Since aging is a natural part of the human experience, we think the content of this book has relevance to the life of each reader. This book is of particular relevance to advanced undergraduate and graduate students, gerontologists, policy makers, program planners, and legislators.

Following the introduction by Louis Lowy, the essays may be loosely divided into three areas. Gary Orgel and Elliott Sclar address broad economic and ethical issues relevant to growing old in the United States. Beth B. Hess and Allan R. Meyers focus on two often neglected groups of aged—women and ethnic minorities. Stanley M. Grabowski and Ruth H. Jacobs discuss the relatively unexplored areas of education and social change in old age, while the bleaker side, institutional care, is limned by Elizabeth W. Markson. Finally, Robert Morris reflects on the realities of the allocation of resources to the elderly in an inflationary economy and proposes policy directions.

The majority of prefaces conclude with thanks to people who made outstanding contributions to the publication of the book. In this case thanks go to the contributors of the chapters herein, for without them there would be no book.

Deep appreciation goes to R. Knight Steel, M.D., director of the Gerontology Center since 1977, not only for his innovation and leadership at Boston University but for his outstanding contributions in health-care programs for the elderly in the broader national and international gerontologic and geriatric communities.

Special thanks go to Marott Sinex and Louis Lowy; as cofounders of the Gerontology Center and as codirectors from 1974 to 1977, they have been instrumental in stimulating enthusiasm about aging and social policy on this campus and nationally.

The Summer Institute in Gerontology, which provided the impetus for this book, came into being due to the foresight, encouragement, and hard work of the Gerontology Center Executive Committee and Boston University Summer Term. Many people at Summer Term have supported our work. Craig Aramian, Donald Dunbar, Margareta Lindstrom, Neil Connell, and Steven Howell are deserving of special appreciation, although others throughout Summer Term have also made great contributions. Members of the Executive Committee include Linda K. Amos, Andrew Dibner, Nina Epstein, Stanley Grabowski, Louis Lowy, John Mogey, Ellen Orlen, Marott Sinex, Marian Spencer, Joseph Devlin, David Hershenson, and Hilda Versluys.

The administration of Boston University, particularly Richard H. Egdahl, M.D., has maintained unwavering support of the Center and its personnel.

Mara Hardy made an outstanding contribution as technical editor of this volume and provided assistance and emotional support throughout. Shirley Levinson, Boston University Gerontology Center Librarian, also provided invaluable assistance.

We should also like to thank Margaret Zusky and Carolyn Yoder, Lexington Books, for their patience and encouragement.

**Public Policies
for an Aging
Population**

# 1

# Introduction

*Louis Lowy*

Social policies are affected by the demographic composition, the level of productivity of a society (be it an industrialized, a preindustrial, or a developing country), the way the social structure operates, assumptions made about human nature, the historical legacy of that society, and the ideologies and value assumptions extant in a society. Policies that social institutions produce reflect the dominance of some values over others, and social problems are defined according to normative conceptions and the degree of tenacity in which they are held. These value choices and definitions of problems are not necessarily derived from agreements by members of that society, nor are they the result of compromises or statements among those persons most affected by them. Societies are unequal in terms of resources to which members have access and the powers that can be brought to bear by various groups and classes. And some classes are in a better position than others to influence a definition of social problems or a determination of social priorities. The aged, for example, may attempt to influence social priorities and resultant public policies, but they are only one of a number of other groups competing for determination of the various priorities and policy choices open to them.

## What Are Public Policies?

Morris defines public policies as

> guides as to the aims of governing to which priorities are assigned and to the means which are acceptable to, or preferred by, a particular government. These guides are general, in that they indicate which problems a government will choose to deal with and which way a government will choose to move when it is confronted with the necessity to take action. In this sense, then, policies are guiding principles for a government. A government may choose a general policy of stressing its citizens' domestic well-being over acquisition of power in foreign affairs. When the well-being depends upon control over external resources, the policy choice is whether to concentrate on domestic resources alone or not. Within such a general policy, a government must decide to what extent it will regulate the acts of its citizens in order to pursue the goal of general well-being, to what extent it will direct its citizens to act in their private capacities to satisfy their own needs; or to what extent it will provide for its citizens' needs directly through government agencies.[1]

1

But policy is not only general, applying to all of government and all of society; it is also specific and sectorial, as some policy may only affect a segment of that society such as the aging population.

### Demographic Trends

As any social policy is affected by demographic distribution of groups, the present demographic changes in our society relative to the aged population are of major import. A few statistics that have relevance for our public social policies in regard to the aging are enumerated here.

At present one in every nine persons in the United States is sixty-five and over, a total of 23.5 million men and women. The proportion of this population varies by race and ethnic origin. Eleven percent of whites, 8 percent of blacks, and 4 percent of Spanish people are sixty-five and over. Between 1900 and 1977 the percentage of the U.S. population aged sixty-five and over more than doubled, while the number increased over sevenfold, from 3 million to 23 million. At the present death rate, the older population is expected to increase 35 percent to 32 million by the year 2000. If the present low birthrate persists, these 32 million will be 12.2 percent of the total population of about 260 million.

In 1900 life expectancy at birth was 48.2 years for white males and 51.1 years for females. For blacks it was 32.5 and 35 years for men and women respectively. A child born in 1976 can expect to live 73 years, about 26 years longer than a child born in 1900. At age sixty-five, however, life expectancy is 16 years; 14 years more for men, but 18 years longer for women. As a result of this sex difference in life expectancy, which begins at birth, there were 146 older women per 100 older men in 1978, and the disparity continues to grow with age. Since people live longer and there are more old people, this fact has tremendous impact on the design of public policies that relate to a sizeable segment of the population. The predominance of a female older population is also likely to point toward designing public policies that have to account for the disparity between the sexes.[2]

Nearly 75 percent of the older males live in a household with their spouse present, compared with nearly 40 percent of women in the same age bracket. Because women enjoy a longer life expectancy, they frequently become widowed while men often remain married until they die. Given the shorter life expectancy, morbidity rates inevitably go up. The number of so-called frail elderly, the most intensive consumers of health and social services, is increasing at a faster rate than the overall number of older persons. Many problems associated with old age in our society, such as low income, loneliness, and poor health, are generally rooted in the overrepresentation of widowed and unmarried females. The longer life expectancy also means adding more generations to family networks, and the four-generation family is no longer a rarity. Considering the economic changes and increasing scarcity of natural resources that this country is undergoing and a greater demand on the part of many segments of the population for their share of the natural resources, it is likely that the elderly are in for a squeeze, as Robert Hudson points out in his article "The Graying of the Federal Budget."[3] Already there is a backlash by the general population about the claims by the elderly for their share of the public dollar. The prevalence of *agism* in our society, a subtle form of discrimination based on myths, stereotypes, and unfounded assumptions about the aging population, is likely to be increasingly fueled by this backlash.

**Origin and Foundations of Social Policies**

Social policies, notably public policies toward the aging, have moved away from reliance on primary kin or filial responsibility toward greater acceptance of a rightful entitlement of benefits based on past contributions to the society. Policies have moved away from dependence on charitable supports that are stigmatized toward more bureaucratized services that meet individual and family needs. However the gap between policy intent and action is wide. Gerontological knowledge has been utilized insufficiently and sporadically, and the elderly are still given low priority in the allocation of public funds and resources. Over the last forty years, the social-welfare system in the United States has evolved into a patchwork of laws, benefits, programs, and services for older people which are designed to respond to their presumed needs and assist in coping with some of their developmental tasks.

Social welfare functions in relation to meeting needs and solving problems can be divided into three categories: the curative-, preventive-, and enhancement-oriented functions. The curative-oriented function provides for the solution of problems that have occurred as a result of malfunctioning within the person or externally because of environmental factors. These can also be termed therapeutic or adjustmental functions. The preventive-oriented function attempts to meet people's needs before they have become problems; consequently, human needs have to be identified well in advance. Enhancement-oriented function advances the social standard for older people by reducing risk conditions that beset old age in order to achieve the highest level of physical and social functioning of which a person is capable.

Enhancement orientation is in accord with a developmental rather than a residual view of welfare. Our system is mostly concerned with alleviating existing intra- and interpersonal problems and helping people cope with conditions in their environment as best they can. This is based on the assumption that the later years are an ipso facto problem condition rather than a normal period in the human life cycle. This perspective looks at the aging population as one beset with problems and defines them as a social problem rather than as a social group. Our youth- and work-oriented society, while ignoring if not rejecting the aged, has created situations that call for new approaches to meet the needs of its aging population. This is why a nonstigmatized network of health and social services is needed to reduce the vicissitudes of old age and assist the aged in solving the normal problems of living that essentially are not of their making.

The foundations of public policies regarding the aged were laid in 1935 with the passage of the Social Security Act and its subsequent amendments that were designed to provide a minimum economic base for a population that was getting older. The Social Security Act, however, has to be understood within the context of a mandatory retirement policy from the world of work. Not until 1978 has the arbitrarily fixed age of sixty-five been extended to the likewise arbitrary age of seventy. Congressman Claude Pepper's efforts to extend the mandatory retirement age is a step in the direction of the full elimination of all mandatory retirement policies. This development occurs as public policy makers are realizing that the financing of the Social Security Act must be rethought. Originally viewed as a contributory insurance program, it has become increasingly recognized that this view, still maintained in the United States in contrast to most other countries, has been more myth than reality. The public is increasingly accepting that the wage-related provisions no longer suffice to support a payment mechanism that has to take into account an increasing number of older people who live longer and therefore make greater use of social insurance benefits. The use of general tax revenues would tap those resources generated by the economy that are not wage related, such as profits from property ownership and stock market yields.

## Economic Policy

The issue of economic support of an older population is not only fiscal but also political. It is a question to what extent our society is willing to redistribute its economic resources to make it possible for older people to retire in dignity and reasonable comfort. The combination of three societal trends, the demographic, economic, and elderly employment, could seriously threaten the elderly's income security and the financial viability of the government support programs. Although the present income program structure has reduced poverty among the elderly, poverty is still disproportionately high. Moreover, this present structure does not assure that during the later years of life an aged person will be able to maintain a standard of living equivalent to that enjoyed earlier in life. While it is true that persons retiring today are relatively better off than their predecessors, even at age seventy retirement still significantly increases the probability of severe income loss, decline in living standard, and impoverishment for many persons. And that probability increases the longer inflation continues at high rates, even calculating the worth of in-kind benefits on income (Medicare and Medicaid, for example). The Supplemental Security Income (SSI) program is a policy instrument providing some guarantee of a minimum income protection by supplementing low social security benefits for older people who meet the conditions of a means test. However, SSI needs major changes with respect to payment levels, employment incentives, and asset limits before it can be considered to offer an adequate floor of a guaranteed income.

In chapter 3 Elliott Sclar discusses the economic and political contexts of aging and economic development, their impact on an aging population, and reviews these issues as they pertain to the present and immediate future.

## Health Policy

Health policy must take into account those problems that distinguish older people from the nonelderly. The concern is not only with the elderly's access to treatment for specific illnesses but also with their need for a full array of health-related services that will help them remain in as good health as possible and in the mainstream of community life. In addition, sufficient resources have to be secured for nutrition, health education, and biomedical research. The means for coping with chronic illness have to be developed, and serious diseases that disproportionately affect older persons have to be prevented. There are two major obstacles to promoting improvements in the elderly's health. One is the widely held belief that all the care needed can be supplied through the present system of medical care. The second is the escalating cost of medical care and the country's limited resources. Today's system of health care is mostly dictated by a medical ideology of the short-term cure. This is more applicable to a younger population; an older population demands long-term care. Therefore, it does not make sense to devote an increasing proportion of the country's health resources to medical treatment of illness on a short-term basis when the growth of the elderly population demands a greater concern for long-term care. As Kane and Kane state: "Health practitioners are continually admonished that they must minister to the whole person. Nowhere is this proviso more relevant than in the care of the elderly."[4] They also indicate that the nursing home as an all-purpose solution to health problems of the elderly has in itself created a set of iatrogenic problems—increased dependency, depression, and social isolation among the aged in the United States. In this country in contrast to several European nations, institutional care of the elderly is conceived of and financed as medical-health service rather than social and health service, despite the fact that institutional placement provides a social context for an individual and constitutes a social intervention.[5]

Health-care costs for the elderly rose from $8.2 billion in 1966 to $35 billion or 29 percent of the nation's total health-care bill in 1977; an increase of 190 percent in real dollars. Before Medicare was enacted in 1966, 15 percent of health-care expenditures was attributable to nursing-home costs; by 1977 that proportion had risen to 20 percent. Although those over sixty-five use a disproportionate amount of almost every type of medical care available, the nursing home is still the form of service most associated with long-term care of the aged. At any one time only about 5 percent of the elderly population live in nursing homes, but it is estimated that over 25 percent of the deaths of those over sixty-five occurred in nursing homes or during brief hospital admissions from a nursing home facility.[6] What is needed is the recognition that a whole array of health-care services including home care, day care, respite care, foster-care programs, and sheltered and protective services are needed to deal with the impaired elderly. This task requires planning on a number of fronts. Institutional long-term care can be organized more as a special service with an important health delivery component rather than the reverse, as is now the case. A well-developed home health program does not obviate the need for high-quality institutional care, but a range of options for patients and their families have to be developed rather than just a single all-purpose solution. The federal challenge is to provide adequate inducements to insure the care of the elderly, no matter what kind of health-insurance program proposals or health-care mechanisms are introduced in Congress.

A restructured health-care system should include such components as adequate alternative facilities for those who lack families, a range of facilities and alternatives to the hospital and nursing home including home care, and innovative and compassionate ways of caring for the terminally ill outside the hospital or nursing home. (The use of hospices is a promising beginning, and the federal demonstration project initiated late in 1979 is a step in this direction.) Elizabeth Markson discusses in chapter 8 several aspects of this policy issue and offers new perspectives on a subject that has been distinguished more by emotion than reason.

## Social Service Strategy

The Older Americans Act, enacted in 1965 and amended in 1978, provides for an array of social services. As Carroll Estes has argued, politics, economics, and social structure have far more to do with the aging process than the biological and physiological changes that occur in the later years of life.[7] "These two ideologies, separatism and pluralism, are at the core of American social policy for the aged...."[8] They have had a major effect on public programs. She points out that the various programs, such as Social Security, Medicare, Medicaid, food stamps, housing, Title XX, social services, and the Older

Americans Act itself, have not met the needs of the elderly as "the policies are largely symbolic and reflect dominant perspectives about the aged. They tend to segregate the aged, often with the poor, as a special class in society."[9] She goes on to say, "The Older Americans Act reflected the growing visibility of interest groups for the elderly and the awakening of academic, recreational and social work professionals to a new field of work."[10] During the economic crises of the 1970s, funding for services was shifted from the federal level to the decentralized network of state units and area agencies on aging under the Nixonian New Federalism. By assigning these agencies the responsibility to look for local resources coupled with diminished federal financial handouts, it was hoped that the growth of federal economic commitments could be minimized. In the late 1970s, the policies began to shift again, abandoning the conception of the social definition of the problems of the aged, and viewing them as an at-risk population whose individual members have diminished capacities that need support.

The impact of the use of community services on the self-concept is elaborated in chapter 2 by Gary Orgel, who looks at the relationship between utilization of services and the dignity of the aging person. His philosophical perspective lends a poignant note to this hitherto ignored theme.

## Older Women and Policy: Ethnic Differences and Programs

Older women are a majority of the aging population. By the year 2000 they will represent 60 percent of those over sixty-five. As the seventy-five-and-over and eighty-five-and-over segments grow, the proportion of women in these segments will grow even faster because of longer life expectancy. Many older women live alone or with people other than relatives. A large proportion live in poverty and the income they do have tends to come from public programs. Only 8 percent are in the labor force. To help relieve their adverse income situation, older women need opportunities for income supplementation. The creation of such opportunities requires that stereotypes, which have been barriers to their employment, be changed, nontraditional work schedules like flexi-time be implemented, and economic disincentives, such as Social-Security earnings limitation, be removed. Finally, the public and private retirement systems, first and foremost Social Security, must be reshaped so that women contribute as equals and derive benefits equal to those of men. In addition to the economic problems, older women must deal with a host of social and psychological problems. Widowhood, and divorces and separations late in life leave many groping for an independence they are ill equipped to pursue. Programs that are designed to assist older women who find themselves in such situations must be developed and funded. Beth B. Hess elaborates on these particular aspects of public policy issues in chapter 4.

## Impact of Race and Ethnicity

The aging population is anything but homogeneous. Not only are older persons differentiated by sex and various ages, they are also differentiated by their backgrounds, notably by race and ethnicity. Only recently have studies on black elderly been reported and implications for public policies been discussed.[11] The double jeopardy effect on nonwhite aged has finally entered the consciousness of policy designers, planners, and practitioners. The backgrounds of older people based on their racial and ethnic heritage in a pluralistic society must allow for different responses by public social policies. This is particularly true for immigrants from different groups, such as the elderly who arrived recently from European or Asian countries, as well as those who have grown older here. To what extent do ethnic heritages embodied in cultural values, ideologies, and traditions reflect and affect the view of the aged themselves? To what extent are these aspects truly considered in the design and implementation of public policies? Allan Meyers, in chapter 5, deals with these questions and offers new insights and options.


## Educational Needs

The definitions of aging as a social problem and the aging population as a population-at-risk have led to public responses in terms of social and health services, means-tested economic measures, or other residual programs. Without denying the problematic aspects of aging or minimizing the importance of providing for meeting the legitimate social, psychological, economic, and political needs of the elderly, the cultural and educational needs that continue throughout life must not be forgotten.

The term *quality of life*, which originated in France and has gradually entered the lexicon of America, applies to the aging as well as to any other age group. Lifelong education, especially during the leisure years does enhance mental and physical well-being.[12] The opportunity to acquire new skills and knowledge is important for older people to cope with societal and technological changes, prepare for reemployment, and remain actively engaged in the affairs of state. To date, however, government has generally ignored the older adult learner. Less than 1 percent of the $14 billion the federal government spends on education for persons past compulsory school age is allocated for persons forty-five and over. The Higher Education Act's lifelong learning provisions need to be strengthened and appropriate funding made available to implement them. Lifelong learning should be redirected into work-and-retirement related areas, but any new adult-learner program should be coordinated with resources that already exist. To help assure the elderly of equality of educational opportunities, financial assistance should be made readily available to them. At the present time education money is used mostly to educate and train service providers. Virtually none is allocated to preventive education to help the elderly care for themselves or training programs that would help them remain active in society. The training needs of those providing services to the elderly will increase; however, what is also needed is a review of public policy regarding education for older adults. Education for lifelong learning should not only be perceived from a utilitarian standpoint but also from a leisure-role perspective. Such a role can be validated if education is made a liberating force for people in their later years to enable them to use their creativity for the benefit of themselves, the young, the middle-aged; in short for the whole society. Stanley Grabowski in chapter 6 considers this from the point of view of what is and what might be.

## Senior Power

A phenomenon that emerged in the 1960s and continues today is the organization of older people on their own behalf. Grass-roots involvement and social-action commitment can bring about feelings of personal dignity, self-worth, and control over one's destiny and create a deeper sense of accomplishment for a large group of older people. 'Senior power' was a slogan in the late 1960s, and the Gray Panthers are one of the most significant illustrations of the translation of this slogan into practice. Their statement of purpose that they are a group of people, old and young, who are together by deeply felt common concerns for human liberation and social change, expresses this particular philosophy well. The question of the politicization of older people and their assertion of their rights, particularly in view of a changing aging population based on differential backgrounds, differential historical experiences, and differential acceptance of their status in society may move us further toward their assertion as a special interest group. Several political scientists, notably Robert Binstock,[13] are somewhat skeptical about the viability as well as the ultimate gains of such organizations. Without minimizing the importance of organizations for those who are involved in them, Binstock and others question whether they are likely to transform American society and provide a significant role for the elderly. Ruth Jacobs elaborates on this subject in chapter 7 and attempts to provide answers to the question she poses.

## The Balance of Public Policies

Robert Morris, a pioneer in social-welfare policy, contributed chapter 9. Through the use of an analytic framework he attempts to answer how a middle ground can be found so the elderly can benefit from universal policies that move from a sectorial to a more inclusive nonsegregated arena. He offers a balance-wheel view and corrects several misconceptions about the direction and resource allocation limits of aging policies. In advocating a national social-welfare policy he projects a plan that is rooted in reality and yet contains a vision of the possible.

The changing demographic and political realities express themselves in continual assessment of public policies toward the aged. The services and income strategy that public policies have designed are likely to come under scrutiny. Answers must be found for such issues as: how to insure that our system of support responds effectively to widely varying circumstances of the elderly and their families; how to make certain that the efforts of government at any level actually enhance and add to the compassionate care and support of families for their elders; how to halt the fragmentation, waste, and duplication that have come with the great proliferation of programs for the elderly at every level of government; how to achieve a simplification of rules and regulations that have erected barriers for older people rather than opened up opportunities for them; how to build partnership with state and local governments to improve the management and delivery of service to the well elderly and the chronically imparied; how to ensure that federally supported programs do not upset existing services for the elderly, especially those in the voluntary sector and those existing in the informal network provided by families, friends, and neighbors.[14]

There is already evidence that the entrance of federal programs into the community causes the exit of other programs or volunteer efforts. How can we build incentives into our system of care that would encourage appropriate responses in each case? How can we guarantee the right of elderly citizens to choose their own alternatives? By what mechanisms shall individual needs be measured or provider services be created? These are just some of the few questions that come with increasing bureaucratization of what Carrol Estes has called "the aging enterprise."

### The Elderly as a Resource

Too often have we looked at the older population as one in need of support, rather than as a group that has a great deal to contribute to themselves and others. As consumers and producers of goods and services they constitute an economic resource. In the political arena they are exercising their political responsibilities as vital and active citizens. In the social sphere they act as providers of services as professionals and paraprofessionals and as volunteers in many programs that link the old with the old and the old with the young. In educational programs, from kindergarten to postdoctoral programs, in private and public institutions, older adults as learners and teachers act as examples and communicate their lifelong experiences, their wisdom as well as their follies, gained in having lived sixty, seventy, or eighty years.

As a psychological resource in what Butler calls "elder function," they transmit values and traditions of the society to subsequent generations, act as role models for the young by teaching them how to grow older and make positive use of that stage of life with dignity and integrity that makes each life cycle unique, worthwhile, and meaningful.

This book brings together the ideas of a number of people in the field of gerontology who have thought about these issues, problems, and concerns, who have raised questions and tried to find answers, worked with older people and their families, been involved in designing and implementing public social policies, and who above all have evidenced a commitment to the continuing well-being of our aging population as part of our total population immersed in efforts to participate in the mainstream of society.

## Notes

1. Robert Morris, *Social Policy of the American Welfare State* (New York: Harper and Row, 1979), p. 17.

2. U.S. Department of Health, Education, and Welfare, Administration on Aging, no. (OHDS) 79-20006, *Facts About Older Americans*. (Washington, D.C.: Government Printing Office, 1979).

3. Robert Hudson, "The Graying of the Federal Budget and Its Consequences for Old-Age Policy," *The Gerontologist* 18(1978):428-440.

4. Robert Kane and Rosalie Kane, "Care of the Aged: Old Problems in Need of New Solutions," *Science* 200(1978):913.

5. Ibid.

6. Ibid.

7. Carroll L. Estes, *The Aging Enterprise* (San Francisco: Jossey-Bass, 1979), pp. 1-15.

8. Ibid., p. 4.

9. Ibid., p. 223.

10. Ibid., pp. 223-224.

11. U.S., Department of Health, Education, and Welfare, *Aging*, (entire issue) September-October, 1978.

12. See Max Kaplan, *Leisure: Lifestyle and Lifespan* (Philadelphia: W.B. Saunders Co., 1979), for an overview of the leisure role and its implications for gerontology.

13. Robert Binstock, "Aging and the Future of American Politics," *The Annals of the American Academy of Political Science* 415(1974):199-212.

14. Ethel Shanas, "Family Kin Networks and Aging in Cross-Cultural Perspective," *Journal of Marriage and the Family* 35(1973):505-511.

# 2

# Self-Concept and the Use of Community Service: Activity and Dignity in Aging

*Gary Orgel*

Some time ago one of my students presented me with a problem in a medical ethics course that I was teaching. After an initial, mild heart attack, a seventy-eight-year-old widow, who kept her own apartment and was otherwise in good psychological and physical health, told her doctor and two daughters that she did not want any treatment if she had another attack and was unable to speak for herself. When she did have the second attack and was unconscious, the daughters consented to an operation intended to implant a pacemaker. The operation was a "success." The patient lived, recovered, and was furious and depressed.

While the class was debating the legitimacy of the daughters' consent, it became clear to me that this was not the real problem. Focusing on the issue of consent reduced a broad and complex social and ethical issue into the far more simple legal and ethical issues of contract. What are the conditions for the possibility of such an attitude on the part of this woman? I am not asking a question about suicide although some would argue that the actions of the seventy-eight-year-old woman are the moral equivalent. I suggest that the motives, emotions, and expectations that contributed to this woman's decision to ask not to be treated are quite different in some important respects from those who contemplate or succeed in committing suicide. Yet had this woman's wishes been carried out and had her death been the result, it would hardly be appropriate to call it a natural death. The problems raised by this woman's story lie somewhere in the gray and fuzzy area between suicide and death that is not presently avoidable by human means. Now one quarter of all suicides in this nation occur amongst persons over sixty-five years of age. That is a statistic alarming in itself. But how many more deaths among older adults are of this hidden nature, and why do they occur?

I will address the contrast between the expectations of Americans, and older Americans in particular, and the human and social realities of American life. The dissonance between expectations and realities is the root of the problems posed by the woman mentioned at the beginning of this chapter, and the solution to these problems is grounded in a transformation of contemporary social realities in America. It might be said that Americans are simply naive and unrealistic, and therefore it is not reality but expectations that must be altered. After all, is that not precisely what is being asked of us with respect to oil and energy in general? Americans are asked to tighten their energy belts instead of insisting on more from the oil companies. After all of our expectations surrounding the use of the automobile have been elevated, we are asked to cut back. Those who demand that only a change of expectations, not a change of social reality, is necessary must answer to the charge that it is they who have offered us the idea of successful living in America. It is they who are at the forefront of those who believe that each of us, if we work at it hard enough, can succeed in America. Happiness is a possibility in America for every citizen willing to work for it, and neither the government nor the economic system shall be obstacles to that happiness. In fact they are both heralded as the great facilitators, although different people stand behind the political and economic institutions in different ways and to varying degrees. What I suggest is that American principles be taken seriously. To do so, however, means that American reality be altered to conform to those principles, and I conclude with some suggestions for such alterations on behalf of the older adult American.

It has been said that there is nothing morally relevant about age itself. In one sense this is quite true. There must be the same kind of fundamental moral commitments to all humans regardless of age. These commitments to the person-in-general prove to be of a wholly negative kind. That is, the kind of moral commitments that apply to persons in general are of the sort "Thou shalt not murder, rape, assault, and so forth." They all embody abstentions from interference with the ongoing life of another in very definite ways. We know, within the limits of any given cultural context, just what "murder" or "assault" or "rape" means. Burning a witch or a homosexual, or flogging a Jew was neither murder nor assault in 1492 in Christian minds. In the 1940s wife beating was declared by the Supreme Court of the United States to be a legitimate form of discipline, and the question still has not been resolved by the Court as to whether a man can rape his wife. Child abuse is still distinguishable from occasional spankings. Yet for the most part these instances are exceptions, and exceptions that many of us would refuse ourselves the right to indulge in. In general 'Thou shalt nots . . .' are taken seriously and we know precisely what that means. This is not so with positive commands. Positive commands are either not generally applicable to all persons or, if they are, we do not know precisely what they mean. "Love they neighbor and thy enemy" does not tell us what love is. There is nothing in American law and very little in American morality that commands us to give anything to others except money in the form of charity.

It is only positive morality that is age specific. It is specific only with regard to definite sociobiological characteristics attached to any given age. We feel responsible for clothing and feeding babies, educating, and loving them. That the object of our action is an infant is morally relevant, but only when morality is taken in its affirmative sense. For an infant, psychobiological conditions demand a certain level of affirmative moral commitment if we are to be good parents and have a succeeding generation. But it is not essentially biological or psychological conditions that raise the question of moral commitment to the older adult America. It is the social condition of poverty, exclusion, retirement, and loneliness. These conditions are created by our own society but are common neither to every culture in our time nor in other times. It is precisely these socially fabricated conditions that in a concrete sense make age morally relevant in a definite way but only in the affirmative sense.

The rationale behind all negative morality of the sort "Thou shalt not . . ." is the basis for an understanding of any positive morality. Negative morality, embodied in our general notion of rights, is held by some to be a sufficient moral code. Others hold that it is a necessary but insufficient moral structure and that something more in the way of positive morality is required of us. Neither group goes far enough. While the second group correctly sees the necessity of going beyond mere restraints or interference in the lives of others, they do not understand or clearly articulate why such an advance is necessary at all. Insofar as human action is undertaken in time, is future oriented, and is aimed at the achievement of some goal, negative morality or the right to be free of interference makes no sense whatsoever unless it is informed and governed by future planning, aspiration, and possible achievement. It is only because I have the possibility of living my life in some manner, that is, acting in some social context, that it makes any sense to demand that my activity be free of restraint. Why would anyone want to be free of restraint if they had no conception of or no possibility of free social action? It is only in order to act, and to act means to engage in a social world, that I demand a limited degree of restraint or interference in my life. In other words all "freedom from constraint" is for the sake of "freedom to engage the social world", that is, to stand in relation to that world and act in it. It is not simply that a life based on negative morality would be cold, impersonal, and isolating; it would also be meaningless. Thus, to the extent that this is precisely the level of moral commitment that we accord to the older adult American, we should not be surprised when they claim and we find that their lives are nasty, poor, solitary, brutish, and short, as Hobbes said of humanity in a state of nature.

The notion, therefore, that negative morality depends on positive morality for its raison d'etre (qua morality) and positive morality presupposes negative morality, leads us to ask just what the role of social aspiration and expectation is in human life or in American life. What 'I am' and what 'I am becoming' have at times been respected and at other times ignored by Western theology and philosophy. Contemporary Americans do not and cannot ignore these issues because they ought not be ignored. But, and this is crucial, both the younger and the older Americans attend to these issues in an essentially negative sense. Neither age group believes any longer either that American society can be reformed or they have a real chance to make something of their lives. A realistic and justifiable lack of faith in the future is rapidly becoming a hallmark of American culture. This attitude cuts across class, racial, and educational lines, as well as those pertaining to age. It is these apparently upwardly mobile, middle-class, college-educated whites together with their lower class and black brothers and sisters who will be the older adult American in thirty-five to forty years. The same thing is heard over and over again in academia: get into the system—make a killing—get out of the system. That the system (whatever that is) suffocates, smothers, and inhibits human development is an attitude popular among all or nearly all strata of society. That one has a chance of getting into the system, sacrificing the opportunity for satisfaction and growth for an allegedly short time, and coming out with money and the possibility of future growth unhindered by institutional constraints is the kind of defensive and naive myth to which only the young, white, or educated can adhere only because at least some from among these groups can succeed on this level. The old, black, or uneducated have little or no reason to believe that these possibilities exist for them.

The popular jargon of "growth experiences," "consciousness raising," "self-actualization," and "developing human potential" in "encounters" and "peak experiences" is a testament to the need of the contemporary American to go beyond who and what he or she is and the reality that social life in general does not afford the average American, let alone the older adult, the opportunity to expand his or her vistas. It is certainly not the case that every human ought to go beyond what he or she currently is. To be a person is to be distinct in space, time, and experience. But it is also and always a function of being a member of a social group from which one learns just what one can or should expect. In this sense the American does not get what he or she expects.

The basis for a critique of American culture does not lie in the fact that all humans ought to have a maximum growth experience in any absolute sense, but in the failure to supply ample opportunity for the achievement of those things that the ideology of this nation says are both desirable and possible. Change in one's life is inevitable. Whether change is in fact also growth is quite another question; growth implies some sort of advance. In this society we have tended to confuse changes in the things around us with growth of either a personal or national kind. Yet in reality growth is always human growth, and the real value of things lies neither in their mere presence nor in their possession but rather in the nature of the effect that their presence or possession has on people. The true test of whether change is actually growth is in the degree to which personal or social life is enhanced. This is tautological and so it seems that without reference to something more there is no way to discern whether growth has really taken place.

In this sense we are again misled by phrases like 'economic growth.' We watch the gross national product increase in volume without any corresponding enhancement of social life in America, and perhaps even a reduction in the quality of that life, while we are told that America has indeed undergone economic growth. Thus the mere increase in the number of things produced, whether money or some other commodity, is sufficient for the public analysts, be they politicians, economists, or journalists, to speak about economic growth. This is an illusory vision, a mystification of human life. But then to what can we refer to establish precisely whether growth or mere change has taken place?

I take there to be at least four possible standards of evaluation in this regard: some transcendant absolute such as a god; some general concept of human nature; the presence or absence of contradictory or conflicting policies, actions, or institutional structures; and subjective beliefs and expectations. Instead of entering the deep debates about religion or human nature, I will point out that we live in a society that attempts to move up and down, right and left at the same time, and consequently social expectations cannot be satisfied. It is for these reasons that Americans, both young and old, have concentrated so much of their energy on inner growth experiences whether they are in psychotherapy, in some newly formed religious cult, or so-called encounter group, which often amounts to little more than a secular cult. This turning inward, however, has significantly different implications for the younger and the older adults. It is in part reflected in the fact that societally growth and aging are regarded as being opposed to one another.

When there is an internalization of energy and attention in college students, this is done in the face of societal structures that nevertheless mandate, even if they do not always facilitate, a turning outward as well. If college-age youth are encouraged to be introspective, it is partly because it is expected that they will utilize the information in the two most significant social and personal relationships into which they will ever enter. We expect first that after college or graduate school they will seek a permanent job, and second that sometime thereafter they will marry and raise a family. These are also expectations that college-age youth have for themselves. What occurs as a result of this is a reciprocal interaction between inwardness of attention and social expectations. In part it is just the anticipation that institutional involvements will inhibit personal growth that produces the turn inward in the first place. The road ahead is regarded by young people as a series of obstacles, a mine field through which they must walk. Involvement in economic institutions is regarded as an unfortunate necessity but a necessity nevertheless. The choice of careers is regarded as a closing of options. In this society the division of labor has produced a one life-one career condition. Thus what one chooses at age twenty-two is regarded as the final choice with regard to productive activity. This finality in itself is viewed as being in direct conflict with the now highly developed value of personal growth, although logically it need not be. It is conceivable that such a choice could be a choice of a context in which choice was actually expanded. The choice of a career could be an event that foreshadowed the opportunity for self-expression, self-development, the exercise of talent, and the fulfillment of social needs.

This period of choice is regarded, and in many ways realistically, as a time when bureaucratic and authoritarian structures will stifle self-expression and development, and talent will be eschewed in favor of conformity to bureaucratic norms. The younger adult in America conceives the process of aging as beginning with Commencement and (rightly) as the end of personal growth. Because a job choice is necessary and because it is necessary insofar as one must acquire money in this culture in order to live, the college student correctly infers that it is money that is necessary and not productive activity. Thus if he or she can acquire sufficient money—in a moderate period of time—it can be used in such a way that she or he will be able 'to retire' by age thirty-five or forty. Investment capital is what is sought by the American college student today. Thus we find a very concrete and often very well informed attitude to money and its uses among college students. What we do not find is a recognition that only some of them will be able to make it and then get out of "the system." This should be a source of major concern for us. Many of today's twenty-five-year-olds will be very frustrated at forty.

Thus turning inward, the focus on the strength of the self, is a product of this view of bureaucratic and authoritarian economic structures in society. But this effect is also a cause. Once personal development is viewed as impeded by institutional structures, all formally designed interpersonal relations are regarded as threatening. Marriage is just such a structure. With it comes definite legal responsibilities, which are regarded as constraints. But if involvement in economic institutions is unambiguously defined in terms of restrictions on personal development, the attitude toward marriage is one of ambivalence. On the one hand, the relationship is regarded as an interpersonal phenomenon wherein the spouse is viewed as a vehicle for self-expression and development. On the other hand, accountability and responsibility to children and spouse is seen as constricting, and this is not diminished by the increased availability of divorce. The divorce option is one in which, with few exceptions, the woman can expect to be primarily and solely responsible for raising the children; the man can expect to be financially responsible in often an economically devastating way for providing for his ex-wife and children. The younger adult knows this and increasingly has come to know that her or his chances of divorce are one in two. The younger adult thus feels increasingly subjected to chance. Nothing appears to be in his or her control except the inner life. Economic institutions appear as Gargantuan vacuums prepared to strip each person of his or her different and distinct abilities. Marital relationships offer a fifty-fifty chance of success, but it is modified by the fact that all social commitments are regarded as personally restricting. The society grounded in individualism and competition is grinding to an interpersonal halt to the same extent as the real relationships and individualism bred by this culture are incommensurate.

I have explored the economic-marital complex as it affects the younger adult American for several reasons. First, these are the people who will be the most educated group of older citizens in the world within thirty-five years; they will expect more and, if present conditions are an indicator, get less. Second, their belief systems are either a result of or will affect the belief systems of older adults. The current value on personal growth stands opposed to attitudes about the ability of institutional structures to act as vehicles for that growth. Americans, young and old, regard institutions—and economic institutions in particular—as significant obstacles to human development. This is evident in the attitude of the college student who is interested in and expects to retire at thirty-five or forty as well as in the middle-class person between fifty and sixty who is living in Florida, Arizona, or California after voluntary retirement. This should lead us to question whether a mere extension of the retirement age or even its elimination will solve any but the most immediate and short-term problems. Nevertheless, some form of institutional alteration is necessary if we are to eliminate the conflict between the value of personal growth and the reality of institutional life. This kind of conflict has resulted in a studying of the self in both younger and older adults and has produced what has been called the culture of narcissism. This obviously has dramatic implications for our present and future moral life.

The conflict has different implications for older adults than for younger adults. The younger adult may place considerable value on personal growth as an inner experience. Yet this same person is necessarily called on to make certain commitments and choices about engaging economic institutions or a spouse. The younger adult is forced by social necessity to become involved in the lives of others. The case is precisely the reverse for the older adult in America. Where the younger adult is about to enter an economic institution, the older adult is being asked to leave it. Where the younger adult is preparing to embark on family life, the older adult at best has the sole relationship of a spouse and at worst is completely alone as a result of divorce or the death of a spouse. It is no wonder that loneliness is the characteristic so frequently cited in discussions about the older adult in America. The value placed on personal growth as an inner experience rather than a social phenomenon is matched on the interpersonal and sexual levels by the reduction of the family unit to its smallest possible number: two people. Historically polygamy became monogamy, but a monogamy vastly different than we know today. Formerly one did not merely marry one other person. One married into a family and could expect both support from that group and personal responsibility for its members.

Many writers currently stress the notion that in policy planning for the older adult, governmental decisions ought to be designed to reinforce familial structure. What these writers ignore is that family structure and capability is not what it used to be. First, economic conditions are such that a man and a woman who have two children can just barely afford to provide for them without the additional responsibility of caring and providing for perhaps as many as four older adults. Second, economic need has given rise to economic mobility not in the monetary sense but in the geographic sense. A young couple, with or without children, must be—and frequently is—prepared to move to whatever part of the country in which gainful employment can be found. A young worker cannot be both responsible for her or his parents as well as for her or his spouse and children. To support his children, a young worker must often move to a city or even a state far removed from his parents. Current welfare legislation is largely a matter of determinations made in and by individual States. In the absence of both a massive restructuring of the economic system and a concentration of greater control over welfare policy in the federal government, it is rather futile to pretend that political decisions could significantly bolster familial relations. This is not to suggest that one ought to ignore the effect on family structure when one is making government policy but rather that broader socioeconomic realities must provide the context for such policy making. In this regard voluntary incentives, like larger income tax exemptions, could be provided for those who have dependent children as well as dependent parents. Massive coercive measures that would present young adults with the option of supporting their parents or letting them starve are, however, inappropriate, and in the long run will not be successful. Government can create the conditions for the possibility of the growth of emotional ties and responsible attitudes. It cannot accomplish this task by creating a socioeconomic vacuum that will force specific people together.

This privatization of both personal growth as an inner phenomenon and the familial experience as a relationship with one significant peer has very extensive social and moral implications for young and old alike, now and in the future. On the one hand, the socialization of children is grossly restricted. The number of people responsible for care of and teaching the young has been diminished. This is further diminished by divorce. While one or two parents no doubt can be caring and loving and wise in relation to their children, as role models they can provide the child with only the most narrow conceptions of social options. The extent, moreover, to which they do act as role models is conditioned by the fact that as the numbers of people responsible for child rearing diminishes, the proportionate degree of responsibility assumed by each adult increases. Thus there is greater stress and complexity in being a "good" parent today than ever before. When a child has two parents, four grandparents, several aunts, uncles, or great aunts and uncles around them, they can learn a myriad of social responses in terms of effectiveness, morality, and emotional expression. As a nation we consistently produce all kinds of psychological and educational theories, arguing that a child who sees many rather than few colors or who hears many rather than few rich musical presentations is more likely to creatively select and produce his or her own aesthetic experiences as he or she gets older. Why have we apparently missed the fact that the same is true in terms of social behavior?

The other side of the privatization of the family and its diminution to a mere two people has, however, its most devastating effects at the other end of the life spectrum. Here we find first that social and broader familial responsibilities are systematically taken out of the hands of older adults. This is not a mere matter of individual choice—young adults selectively stripping older adults of their influence over children—based on fancy and whim. It is rather an exclusion based on the specific forms of economic and social need experienced by the average, contemporary young adult. The older adult is from one perspective just another nonproductive mouth to feed, and because economic productivity measured in dollars is the standard by which one measures the value of an adult, these older adults are regarded as children in adult bodies long before they are senescent. But even if the older adult is actually economically productive, the privatization of the family has made it a cultural anomaly to value these outsiders. Two women under one roof is impossible. The family patriarch sits at the head of the table only at Christmas. The grandparent who, only thirty years ago, was still an active role model for grand-children and participant in familial decision-making has become a visitor who lives in New York, Tennessee, or California. The removal of the older adult from this context strips them of precisely that kind of responsibility that this society simultaneously proclaims to value. The grandparent was once an important mediator in family development, a sieve through which parent-child conflict could pass in order to bring an experienced perspective to the issue at hand. As a society we still claim to value this experience, if not in the marketplace, at least in the home. Thus, we produce in the older adult the expectation that this is their appropriate social role.

At the same time, however, we deny older adults access to the context in which they might carry out these responsibilities. It is unfortunately not quite as simple as this. At the same time that we claim to value their experience, we proclaim that retirement entails an escape from children, their noise, mischief, dirty diapers, and torn jeans. Numerous lawsuits have already been brought by angry cooperative and condominium owners in the so-called retirement states for bringing children into their adult paradise. The older adult is a confused person, not senile, but in harsh value conflict about precisely what his or her responsibilities ought to be. Calling on the experience of the older adult is in direct conflict with the possibility of exercising the responsibility of guiding children and the right of the retired person to be left alone. As usual in America, the only value that is not in conflict with reality is this right to be left alone. Singularity and individualism continue to prevail in the most competitive, internally warlike nation in the world. It is not only that older adults are lonely. In some sense they demand to be left alone. It is not the case that their loneliness is a mere product of neglect. It is also a direct product of the individualism that they taught us and still espouse. Loneliness is the logical correlate of individualism and is as easily and frequently located among twenty-year-olds as seventy-year-olds. Refashion the socioeconomic conditions that produce and require the ideology of individualism and embark on a path that could lead to the dissolution of loneliness or hold onto these socioeconomic structures and guarantee your own isolated future.

Not only do these conflicts in values and between values and reality contribute to the production of loneliness, but they also produce the feeling of irresponsibility as well as the actual inability to act responsibly. The older adult finds himself or herself in a position of being unable to act responsible just because he or she is unsure of just what responsibility is. Thus the older adult comes to be viewed as socially irresponsible, although this takes the form of an attitude to economic and social productivity. The social role that older adults traditionally played is still valued to some degree. The opportunity to play that role is denied them. When one cannot fulfill the social role designed for and accepted by them, social irresponsibility is the unfortunate but necessary result.

It is in one sense inaccurate to suggest that the older adult is unable to fulfill any major social function. The privatization of the family and personal growth do result in at least one significant relationship and that is with one's spouse. In this nation the spouse has become the only significant peer with whom the older adult has a definite relationship. In conjunction with this is the expectation that each spouse will be responsible emotionally, economically, and technically, in the home for the life of the other. In one's later years it is expected that on these levels one person will meet these social needs. Gone is the support that came from other family members and children when the couple was young. The older adult couple is freed from these ties and responsibilities and set adrift alone to make its way in the socioeconomic world. This necessarily produces considerable reliance on the spouse for the satisfaction of social needs. It is now the time to relax together, get to know each other again, and care for one another. Freed from responsibilities to other family members and economic institutions, all attention can now be focused on one's spouse. Our romantic notion of love has its fulfillment in bringing these two persons together once again for one final period of time, unhindered by any other social demands placed on them. Now the couple is placed in a position to reinforce those things that they have always known. The spouse, the person who knows you better than anyone else, with whom you have shared most if not all of your inner feelings, has for these reasons become the sole vehicle for self-expression.

Over the years you have developed your values, interests, and needs together so that the fulfillment of these in one person is simultaneously one's fulfillment in the other. This one relationship, among all others, has been forged as it had to be on the basis of cooperation. You are no longer confined, as you were when you were younger, by institutions external to the marital bond. No employer or employee, no children or family make demands on you. You are detached from, and therefore what you give to, the outside world is wholly a matter of your choice as members of a couple. The fear and anger about institutional entanglements that pervaded your life when you were younger are gone. The obstacles to personal growth and self-expression have been removed, and if you had once been wary even of making a commitment to another person, this too is gone. If inner personal development was all you really had faith in when you were young, you are at least now content that, within the limits of your abilities, you have gone outside your self and done something with another person. Here the successes and failures that you count are not merely the products of your inner life, your personal ambition, your own fortitude, but they are the successes and failures of two people acting as a couple. The original faith in the mere inner life of personal growth has, in a world of billions of persons, made some slight concession. You now know that it is possible to move through and grow in the world around you with at least one other person. You know this because within certain limits you have done it. You have conceded, whether you are conscious of it or not and regardless of the extent to which it occurred, that personal growth is something more than a mere inner phenomenon that you experience. It has become in part something that occurs in the world and between you and another. You have learned life's lesson. And what a harsh education it has been. No one made it easy for you. For the last forty years, every obstacle imaginable has been thrown in your way. Luck and strength, or perhaps fear, has brought you this far together.

The original mistrust of social institutions has remained intact. If you prefer to work rather than retire, it is not because the marketplace is no longer a mine field but rather in spite of the fact that it is. What has changed in an ever so slight manner is the conviction that personal development is a matter of the inner self. At least there is one's spouse. At least there are the events, experiences, feelings, successes, and failures of the last forty years that bespeak the fact that if he or she had not been there, "My life would have been less fulfilled." This one single person is the flickering or shining star in a nation devoid of people who truly have your interests at heart. From being a single person you moved to being a couple and thence to being a parent only to return to being a mere couple. But you know that only the luckiest will die together. The death of one before the other is a virtual certainty. So you know that either being single or dying lies ahead for you. Having put all your inter-personal eggs in the basket of your spouse, one or the other will be the return on your investment. Moreover you and your spouse do not have equal chances in this regard. You know that probably only she will ever be single again. The occupation-marital complex finally resolves itself into women's retirement villages and female nursing homes where the men are few in number and have little in common with all these strangers. The male-dominated marketplace is turned on its head, and older adults return in droves to our own version of the matriarchal cave constructed by our anthropological forebears thousands of years ago.

If limited responsible action is the hallmark of the final stage of your married years, only leisure, care, and treatment reign after separation by death. Of course there are many variants here. Some will remarry. Some will live together and break with values that may be eighty-five years old in order to collect double social security. The number of ways in which retirement followed by the death of a spouse is resolved is, however, not nearly as great as the number of individuals confronted by these circumstances. Most will follow a similar path, again dictated by family structure and economics. This path of loneliness, this time when at best you are a member of a mere couple and at worst you are a single person among other single persons, is the meager inheritance of the older adult. It is an inheritance bequeathed to them in part by their own passive acceptance of structures and values that promote consumerism and individualism and by our commitment to those same phenomena. If leisure and retirement are equated with isolation and loneliness, it is only because socially productive activity is seen as an obstacle to and not as a vehicle for personal growth in our society.

Moreover, this vision is not a mistaken one. It is a conceptual mirroring of the present social reality. Yet this is only the negative side of the social coin. In the face of mistrust for social institutions and a reliance on inner growth as personal growth, the younger adults were faced with the necessity of engaging in coordinated institutional activity and marital relations. This brought them to the limits of interpersonal self-realization in marriage after the departure of their children. Loneliness was forestalled by institutionalized socioeconomic activity and interdependent action with a spouse. Contemporary focus on provision of leisure time for and care and treatment of older adults simply is a way of ideologically justifying the developmental limits of the person in our country. Given the facts noted already, the question for most analysts is not how to change these conditions but rather how, given these conditions, the passive, older adults can be provided, in the consumerism mentality, with sufficient bases for a minimally enjoyable series of final years.

The picture painted here is one in which the only real activity that is trusted in terms of personal development is the inner activity of the self. As for social life, Americans regard themselves as the passive recipients (consumers) of the wild and uncontrollable forces of institutions whose structures they have not created and whose actions they do not fully comprehend. Those who envision the older years of these Americans as morally deficient do so in precisely the terms that created the deficiency in the first place. When the status of the older American is discussed, focus is brought to bear on their consumptive needs alone. Most analysts are concerned with whether they have enough money; with whether they receive sufficient and appropriate care and treatment. Certainly these are legitimate questions. They are legitimate, however, only in a limited sense, for in concentrating on them, the truly problematic issues of social activity, social productivity, and meaningful and purposeful social action are ignored. There is no doubt about just why these issues must be sidestepped. If they are confronted then the very bases of American socioeconomic structure would come under scrutiny, and this the apologists for this structure cannot tolerate.

The real problem, a problem that needs to be attacked on every front, is the institutional structure of the socioeconomic world. In one sense those who view these institutions as mammoth hindrances to human development are quite correct. The time has long passed since Americans could be fooled by the notion that the profit motive was consistent or commensurate with motives surrounding real human development. We have learned too much from shortages of sugar, coffee, lettuce, and now oil, too much from double-digit inflation and the rise of the acceptable minimum level of unemployment from 4 percent in 1972 to 6 percent in 1979; all this is in the face of a 26 percent increase in corporate profits from 1978 to 1979. But those who view these statistics in the merely negative sense fail to see that these institutions can be exploited for the purpose of enhancing human development in the United States. It is no doubt the case that technological development has made it not only possible but necessary that fewer and fewer people are employed in the manufacturing realm of the socioeconomic world. Automation is the opposite of employment in this sector. Just for this reason, however, we are becoming a nation of people that focuses, and can focus, more and more on the so-called service occupations. This is particularly fortuitous for the older adult, if we take proper advantage of the phenomenon.

In seeking out avenues for self-expression and continued personal development we must be aware of four things. The first is the kind of expectations and abilities that older adults possess. Here the problem is one of overgeneralization; that is, expectations and abilities are as unique as they are general. Unfortunately, and this is true for all sectors of the populace, we are at a developmental stage in our national history where uniqueness counts very little. Most of us are regarded as, and indeed are, wholly replaceable in our jobs. We are replaceable because by and large it is the general features of our expectations and abilities that are sought after whether we are college professors, doctors, steel workers, or truckers. No doubt uniqueness counts more in some socioeconomic sectors than in others, but these are the exceptions not the rule. We must not simply passively accept this condition but rather understand fully that this is our point of departure and make appropriate decisions about demands that can or should have certain long- as well as short-term consequences.

Second, we must also seek institutional contexts that draw on our general abilities and provide a context for the expression of uniqueness. Institutions that are service oriented provide such a framework for they are the structures most likely to offer the possibility of direct interpersonal contact. Apart from artistic endeavor this is the most poignant way of putting one's stamp of uniqueness on a social action under contemporary conditions. Third, we must take seriously—but reformulate and reapply—the notion that certain socially and personally significant phenomena occur in the family. And finally, we must take cognizance of the fact that the great bulk of funding for such endeavors will come from the federal government. While we should not seek government funds exclusively, it would be appropriate for us to go after those funds vigorously. If federal monies are not used to reinstate the older adult into the mainstream of social life, they will be used to pacify that segment of the population by distributing all sorts of material things to them.

An examination of the traditional social role of the older adult will tell us what older adults were taught to expect when they reached a certain age. Whatever society is considered, we find that the older adult played a significant role in the socialization of the young, both in terms of the passage of social wisdom and the ability to provide care and love. The family no longer provides a general context within which older adults can express themselves in these ways. We should not do anything that would encourage this phenomenon—at least not until other meaningful avenues have been opened. Familial ties will not, however, be made firm again until other major changes take place in the economic world. The contemporary older adult in America cannot wait for these alterations. There are at least two institutions where immediate contacts between American youth and older adults can be established. These are schools and day-care centers. In these contexts the older adult can become responsible for other human beings once again. This is not a mere opportunity to be responsible but an occasion to know yourself as a responsible person. With this knowledge comes several things, not the least of which is enhanced self-respect and a reestablishment of the knowledge of one's self-worth because one has actually become socially important once again. And it is not just the older adult who benefits here. The benefit that accrues to the older adult in this context is a function of and predicated on the benefit that accrues to others. Just as neither doctors nor teachers can benefit qua doctors or teachers unless patients or students benefit, so too gains in feelings of self-respect and self-worth among older adults can only be found where there are concommitant gains in the attitudes of their young charges.

The young are not the only ones who can benefit from the activities of the older adult. Approximately 20 percent of older adults need some kind of care due to their physical disabilities. Many among the remaining 80 percent have cared for spouses or have first-hand experience of disease or trauma themselves. The older adult who cares for another older adult is another source of social participation. There is, however, a hidden danger here. The problem is that the self-respect and social status of the older adult in America has been reduced. This means that even older adults view other older adults as less socially useful, less socially valuable than other members of society. If you do not respect the people you care for or work with you are far less likely to come to respect yourself for caring for or working with them. In so far as we are a "youth culture" we should use that to bolster the self-image of the older adult. We should do this not to the exclusion of the involvement of older adults with older adults but merely in preference to it.

Federal monies are being made available for all of these types of endeavors. The literature indicates that most people do not have the vision to pursue this money for these reasons. Because most analysts and the people who write grant proposals are negatively predisposed to social labor, they are more interested in the benefits of retirement rather than the benefits of continued and perhaps increased social involvement for the older adult. Institutions, moreover, like schools and day-care centers are becoming more and more receptive to the incorporation of the older adult into the daily schedule. While most of these institutions could not provide the funds to do so, they might willingly accept their assistance if it was paid for by a governmental agency. This is now possible. Furthermore, it is not particularly important in a general sense just what the older adult does in these contexts. Certainly there should be consideration given to the age and physical condition of the older person. Generally it may be appropriate to concentrate more on mental and verbal skills than physical skills, but concentration should not be universally restricted in this way. It must be remembered, however, that the vast majority of these older adults will be women. This is partly true because of life expectancy and partly true because we have taught women and not men to be both emotionally sensitive and inclined to community involvement. The kind of commitment desired from the older adult must be a function, to the greatest extent possible, of their specific and unique characteristics, and this means that attention must be paid to gender and the specific historical experiences of particular older adults.

Imagine that the same seventy-eight-year-old woman mentioned at the beginning of the chapter went three times a week to a school where she spent a couple of hours a day interacting with a group of eight-year-olds. Imagine that she had actually come to feel responsible for the social education of these children. While it is possible, is it now as likely that she would refuse treatment and ask to die? Would not the sense of responsibility, the feeling of a new self- and social-worth, mediate this thought? Would she not be more likely to be concerned about just what would happen to these young children if she dies and therefore feel the need and desire to remain with them? Of course, all we can say is that she probably would feel these things. But this woman is the general older adult. How many suicides would we prevent and how many of these hidden deaths if we provided older adults with meaningful social activities? What is now a broad medical ethics problem can become, if we make the commitment, a series of isolated events. These events would no doubt pose ethical problems but would be reduced as much as possible from their presence as a major social dilemma to those of selected, isolated, and minimal number of individual dilemmas. To accomplish these tasks we must take the restrictive, debilitating, and inhuman nature of the socioeconomic system in America far more seriously than we do now.

# 3 Aging and Economic Development

*Elliott Sclar*

Human aging is by definition a phenomenon as old as the human race. The study of it is very recent. In the United States organized efforts to study aging date back slightly over thirty years to the founding of the Gerontological Society. The two major governmental organizations that support scientific inquiry into the aging process and its problems are of even more recent vintage. The Administration on Aging was founded in the mid-1960s and the National Institute of Aging in the mid-1970s, each with a multimillion-dollar budget. Given the agelessness of the problem, the question of why such recent increase in social interest becomes very provocative.

The simple answer to that question is a demographic one. There are more older people than ever before. In 1900 only one in twenty-five Americans was over the age of sixty-five (the customary demarcation of elderly status). Presently that figure is approximately one in ten.[1] In other words, the population sixty-five and over has grown 567 percent since the turn of the present century.[2] As with all simple answers, it begs more of the question than it resolves. The fact that there are more older people does not by itself constitute sufficient grounds for the creation of what is perceived as a social matter worthy of a large expenditure of society's resources.

An increased number of older people is only perceived as a problem when a society's institutions are unable to accommodate themselves to the needs of these additional older people. To understand why aging has become a major issue of social concern, it is necessary to look at the problem historically from the perspective of how social institutions do or do not adapt to the aging of the population.

This chapter focuses on the question of the recent interest by looking at the adaptation of social institutions to the needs of the elderly from an economic-development perspective. In the context of the principal literature in social gerontology, this approach represents something of a departure. Social gerontology usually views the problem ahistorically and through the specific context of the problem areas as defined by the traditional social-science disciplines: anthropology, sociology, economics, and political science. For example, economists will generally concern themselves with questions of labor force, pensions, and income distribution; political scientists with those of policy formation and interest group activity; sociologists with matters of demography and social networks; and anthropologists with matters of role and status cross-culturally.[3]

The shortcoming of this approach is that it must fragment the social problem of aging into disciplinary parts in order to achieve indepth analysis. Aging
in society is, however, a total process which is not experientially separable
into previously defined categories. Therefore, unless we have a form of analysis that synthesizes as well as analyzes, it is not possible to create an effective understanding of the possibilities for ameliorating the social problems of
aging through conscious social intervention.

To choose to treat the social salience of aging from the perspective of
economic development represents an attempt to overcome that fragmentation
of analysis. A developmental approach to any social issue must of necessity be
both historic and synthesizing. It is historic because it must be viewed in the
context of change over time. It is synthetic because it must look at the social,
economic, and political institutions of society in the context of one another.

To orient the developmental analysis to economic concerns is not as provincial, in a social-science sense, as might first be thought. The social history
of the United States can be viewed as a series of social adjustments to a series
of transformations in the economy. Starting as a local, self-sufficient cottage-
craft economy, it became a regional factory-based one with local ownership.
It was then transformed into a national and international mass-producing
economy with absentee corporate ownership. At each step along the way,
social and familial relationships underwent drastic change to meet the evolving
labor requirements of this changing economy. Enormous social dislocations
accompanied the movement of populations from rural areas all over the world
to America's urban centers. These dislocations in turn were a major reason
for the growth of social-welfare and public-health organizations and institutions
in the late nineteenth and early twentieth centuries.

The last sixty years of American economic history differed from the earlier
history because the period of rapid growth subsided. As a result the huge
appetite of the economy for labor power diminished. This in turn led to a
closing of immigration with its particular stresses and strains. The structure of
the economy changed from one based on small firms in fierce competition with
one another to one dominated by larger units using more stable pricing patterns.
These two factors contributed to the development of an aging population in
an economy with a more stable demand for labor power. It is this economy
and its institutions that are examined now in order to understand the social
basis for the present concern with the problems of the elderly.

## Present Economic Development and Social Organization

The present stage of American economic development is one in which mass-
produced outputs generated by multinational, multilevel corporations dominate
economic activity.[4] Such economic organization is supported by, and supports,

a large, public bureaucracy and large nonprofit organizations including universities and foundations. Using government statistics on employment combined with data from the *Fortune 500* directories, I estimate that more than 40 percent of the U.S. workforce is presently employed by public and nonprofit organizations. A decade ago only about one-third of the workforce was so employed. Given the increasing trend toward corporate consolidation, there is little reason to expect this process to abate in the near future.

One important effect of this trend is to place increasing pressure on individuals to be geographically mobile if they wish jobs with financial security and career advancement. These job pressures play a major role in the extraordinarily high rates of mobility that characterize American families. Approximately half of American families make a major move every five years. To sustain such mobility for economic purposes requires a more compact social organization of the family. In general this leads to smaller nuclear families with few, if any, community ties.

This tendency has some important implications for older people. The increased mobility demanded of the nuclear units makes it more and more likely that kin will be located at longer distances from one another. According to the U.S. Department of Transportation, approximately half of all intercity travel in the United States is accounted for by individuals traveling for family reasons. The distances between family members are not only geographic, but they tend to become social and psychological as well. As members of kinship networks develop day-to-day life styles that exclude one another, it becomes increasingly difficult for them to adapt to the needs of taking care of one another when the situation is more than a short-term emergency. Since it is frequently older family members in need of care on an extended basis, the geographic, social, and psychological distances create major barriers to the use of family as a source of such care. This adds to the pressures on government and private agencies to provide more care for the elderly.

A concomitance of the process of family nuclearization has been the segregation process. Any metropolitan area one might choose to investigate can be viewed as a conglomeration of neighborhoods and suburbs which tend to be homogeneous on the basis of income, race, education, and age.[5] With respect to age in particular, the degree of residential segregation has increased dramatically over the past forty years.[6] As the family as a primary unit for economic and social organization has diminished over time, people have sought the companionship of generational peers rather than relationships based on familial ties.

Such age homogeneity has both benefits and costs. For example, young families might be more willing to support excellent school systems and older families less willing. Age segregation allows local communities to avoid such age-related political disputes. On the other hand, age segregation robs the community of important social complementarities which not only make life more pleasant but avoid the need to set up some formal service delivery systems.

Older people might need help with errands and home maintenance while younger families frequently need assistance with child care. Age-integrated communities permit the emergence of informal social networks in which such services can be exchanged across the age spectrum as a result of role and reciprocity.[7] Age segregation also forecloses the rich experience of life which day-to-day contact across the age spectrum affords to all community members. This is an especially severe loss from the developmental experiences of the young.[8]

Taken together, nuclearization and segregation play a major role in the formation of the social isolation which many observers have commented on in recent years. However, in addition to such social effects, this isolation also has economic consequences. It accentuates the patterns of highly individualized consumption that characterize social isolation. Lacking networks through which goods and services can be exchanged on the basis of role and reciprocity, socially isolated households are compelled to duplicate one another's range of consumer goods and services. In communities with greater social integration, it is possible to get far more efficient use of existing goods and services. For example, the redistribution of discarded clothing can be organized through family and community networks; Sunday dinners and other communal meals can permit more sharing of food and the tasks of food preparation; expensive items of home maintenance, such as power tools, can be shared by more people with virtually no loss of convenience; services, such as child care and home care, can be provided on the basis of role and reciprocity rather than purchased.[9] Many of the items that comprise the living standard of the elderly could be obtained at a greatly reduced cost in the context of greater social and familial integration.

### Income and Work

The breakdown of social and familial units which the economic development process creates would be a major problem in and of itself in a society with increasing numbers of elderly people. However, the problem is even more severe when it is placed within the context of an economy prone to the creation of surplus labor. With the exception of a few war-time booms, the past five decades have witnessed a long-term stagnation in the ability of the American economy to employ its entire workforce.

While the reasons for this economic stagnation are still a matter of debate among economists and economic historians, one fact is clear. The completion of settlement of the American continent and its basic industrialization have led to an end to the hunger for labor power that characterized the first three hundred years of North American history. As a result, labor demand is generally shaped by the relative expansion and declines of particular industries. However, the rate of growth of the labor force has exceeded that of demand for labor. The result is that jobs are increasingly rationed by a range of nonmarket arrangements. These include educational credentials, union and management agreements, race and age. These arrangements have given birth to a host of labor-market theories that increasingly view the process by which we ration work to members of society as one that is more social and political than economic.[10]

The way in which these decisions are carried out have important implications for all members of society as more than work is rationed by these non-market arrangements. Work is only a means to an end. In this society work is the principal way in which we distribute income and social esteem. Together these constitute the necessary conditions for leading a rewarding and satisfying life. For a variety of reasons beyond the scope of this chapter, a social decision exists to ration work on an age basis in favor of the young.[11]

Whatever its merits, this decision has caused severe deprivations for the elderly. The major reason for the disproportionate amount of poverty among the elderly can be traced to the fact that they are separated from the work-force.[12,13] The creation of social security was a direct political response to this problem. The 1935 Social Security Act is the centerpiece of public efforts to provide services and income to the elderly. However, it provides financial help only if the elderly agree to leave the workforce almost totally.

An important feature of the Social Security Act to its depression-era designers was this retirement test. To be eligible for social security payments, older people are required to be effectively out of the workforce with the exception of an amount of wage income below the poverty line.[14] Any additional income over that amount leads to a reduction in social security benefits of $1.00 for every $2.00 earned. That is equivalent to a 50 percent income tax. For those in the workforce to be taxed at such rates they must have taxable income in the neighborhood of $40,000. The retirement test is only applied to income earned from wages or salaries. There is no limit to the amount of income that an individual receives from other sources. Consequently it is those with the fewest assets and resources who are hardest hit by this provision. It is precisely these individuals who most need the additional income that they can only obtain through participation in the workforce. Yet it is they who are effectively barred. Despite the severe social injustice of the provision, it is permitted to stand as law because it continues to serve its depression-era function of creating jobs for younger workers.[15]

Social Security was vastly improved by the 1972 amendments. It was amended so that benefit levels are automatically adjusted to account for increases in the cost of living. Despite this improvement, Social Security is not designed to provide any more than a floor below which the elderly should not fall in terms of living standards.[16] The exact benefit level at any point in time can be viewed as a political compromise. First, the level must be high enough to prevent serious opposition to the status quo on the part of the elderly and their supporters. Generally this means insuring that the level provides sufficient income so that the elderly do not become socially disruptive because of economic deprivation. At the same time the level must be low enough so that it can be sustained through taxes on the active workforce. As inflation and slowed economic growth continue, this compromise will become increasingly difficult to maintain. As the population of elderly swell in the coming decades, it will only exacerbate this dilemma.

The interaction of the various factors described here, when taken together, produces a very bleak situation. In order to keep the present economic system politically stable, especially in a slow economic growth era, most people are forced out of the workforce at age sixty-five or seventy. Given the nexus of work and income, such a transition is materially difficult. For the vast majority of people retirement means lower income.

It is frequently held that improvement in the economic condition of the elderly can be brought about by continued improvement in the terms of private pensions and social security. Such a view creates the impression that the problem is technical or economic in nature and can be corrected by the proper amendments to the Social Security Act or alterations in the laws governing private pensions. Such changes can be important, especially when there is an inequity with respect to the administration of a benefit program. However, the problem of adequate income for an entire class of people is more than a technical adjustment to a benefit package. To understand why this is so, it is useful to think of Social Security and pension plans as a set of bookkeeping rules. These rules are used to determine the amount of current output that is to be paid to former members of the workforce. The pattern of distribution of current output can be termed a zero-sum game. In such a game, if one group gets more, another must get less. The share that goes to the elderly as a group is therefore governed by social norms pertaining to their value to society. In addition, in times of scarcity and slow growth when all groups are forced to compete more keenly, it is difficult to make any substantive gains in terms of improving the economic conditions of the elderly. Any improvement can only come about as part of a larger political consensus. At present none exists.

In addition to the economic distresses that loss of work creates, there are also psychological ones. People are valued by others in society on the basis of their work roles. Work roles confer not just income but power and prestige on individuals. Further work is an important outlet for our urges to contribute to society and create things of value. Even when sufficient retirement income is available, it is frequently the case that the loss of the work role causes sufficient loss in social esteem to lead to severe psychological and physical distress. This in turn frequently leads to illness and death for many shortly after retirement.[17] Even though we ceased to have adequate work for all wishing it a half-century ago, we still have not devised social-esteem systems that adequately value people in non-work roles. Until we do, this problem of work loss will continue to be a serious one for many segments of our older population.[18]

## The Residential Location of the Elderly

The two major reasons that any person has for remaining in any particular residential location are family and work. Given the process of social isolation, family becomes a less compelling reason for remaining in any particular location. The retirement process acts to cut the other tie. The decision to stay or relocate then becomes one that hinges on factors of locational amenity and income.

A decision to stay in a particular place is one that must, in all probability, be made in the face of social and economic changes that are taking place in that community. Both urban neighborhoods and suburbs are in a continual state of flux. In the nineteen thirties, forties, and fifties these areas were characterized by steady development at the periphery of the metropolitan area and decay at the core. Presently the reverse is more typical. It is happening in a very uneven process however. It varies greatly among American metropolitan areas. Each decision then must be viewed as idiosyncratic in terms of individual needs and area location. In general, however, the options among which the elderly have to choose are usually of the lesser-of-two-evils type unless the individual is wealthy.

The process of change of a neighborhood can be characterized as one in which the area is going from use by a higher to a lower socioeconomic group or as one in just the opposite stage of transition. In either of these situations the elderly are pressured to make a locational decision. If the area is in downward transition, the elderly long-term residents face problems of deteriorating housing, increasing crime, and loss of good public services. The decision to stay in the face of these changes can be a painful one. However, lifelong ties may outweigh the increasing amenity costs. It may also be that a decision to stay comes about because of a lack of economic choice to move. That makes the neighborhood deterioration even harder to bear.

If the area is one in upward transition, it is usually accompanied by an improvement of neighborhood amenities. However, such change is not necessarily hospitable to the older person unable to afford the higher housing costs that remaining in the neighborhood would entail. Those forced out face very traumatic adjustments. Studies of the relocation process reveal that many oldsters die from causes linked to the adjustments necessitated by such a move. The survivors often find themselves in strange settings not of their own choosing.[19]

One option which is frequently seen as better is the movement to a retirement village. Such a move is limited only to those elderly with the necessary savings to be able to make a down payment on a dwelling unit. In general it has much to recommend it. It frequently means relocation to a part of the country with a mild year-round climate. It can also mean the support and companionship of peers in clean and attractive surroundings.

Though such retirement communities have some appeal, they also have serious drawbacks because of a lack of planning. The marketing strategy behind the development of these villages is aimed at portraying a life of leisure for active older people with moderate to high incomes. A difficulty with that approach to the development of retirement communities is that they ignore many important future realities. The elderly, as any other group, are not homogenous in terms of needs and abilities. Neugarten has identified two developmental stages for older people.[20] One stage is characterized by good health and mobility. The second stage is one in which people need a range of increasing health and social services if they are to be maintained outside of institutions.

It is precisely the needs of this latter stage which are ignored in the planning and development of most retirement communities. Such realities do not help to sell a place. However, unless such infrastructure is planned when the community is established it becomes increasingly difficult to graft the necessary services onto it to insure some independence for the residents. As a result such places are proving to be only interim respites. Increasing numbers of people are abandoning their retirement communities and returning to the places they came from despite the difficulties of finding satisfactory accommodations.[21]

At their best, retirement communities create a certain irony. Despite the busy schedule of activities, such places exude a "put out to pasture" quality. To a degree, retirement cuts people off from a connection to society which is viewed as socially vital. Being put out to pasture is effectively another way of institutionalizing people. Despite the attempt to integrate more and more of other groups into society, one of the more humane solutions we have developed for many of the elderly is essentially a form of isolation from the "real" economic and social world.

The problems of the elderly, whether or not they are isolated, become even more difficult when they involve failing physical and mental abilities. As a result of the social segregation imposed by the mobility of the labor force, for many of the elderly there are no families to turn to for help. Help is provided by bureaucracies, be they government, charity, or business administered. Regardless of the provider organization, the economics of the situation are such that these services must be provided by a low-wage workforce.[22] This creates a situation where those workers considered most marginal to the economy provide a service to those people considered most marginal to the society. This situation is inherently an alienating one for both provider and recipient. Rather than have one's needs met in the context of a family and community where there is mutual love and respect, the service is at best a perfunctory exchange between strangers. The more personal the nature of the service needed, the more alienating the interchange.

### Conclusions: The Politics of Improvement

This chapter shows how the demands of the economy for a mobile labor force have exacerbated the problems of the elderly in both economic and social terms.

The point is not to create the impression that the problems cannot be ameliorated because they are part of a larger process. The intention is, in fact, just the opposite. It is to argue that the options for improvement are larger because the arena of forces acting on the elderly are larger than we frequently think based on day-to-day experience. However, if the arena is larger, so are the coalitions that must be formed to create a political atmosphere in which improvements for the elderly are possible. Thus we must go beyond a narrower interest group view of the elderly. We must put forth the idea that the problems of the elderly are everyone's problems. Only in that way will it be possible to obtain both the specific changes in service and income problems to ameliorate immediate problems and the broader changes in economic and social policy to lessen these problems in the future.

## Notes

1. Donald Cowgill, "The Aging of Populations and Societies," *The Annals of the American Academy of Political and Social Science* 415(1974):1-18.

2. In absolute terms the growth is from just over three million people in 1900 to approximately twenty million in 1970. Source: Jacob S. Siegal, "Some Demographic Aspects of Aging in the United States," in *Epidemiology of Aging,* eds. Adrian M. Ostfeld and Don C. Gibson, DHEW pub. no. (NIH) 75-711 (Washington, D.C.: Government Printing Office, 1975), pp. 17-82.

3. See, for example, Robert H. Binstock and Ethel Shanas, eds., *Handbook of Aging and the Social Sciences* (New York: Van Nostrand Reinhold, 1976). It is an excellent collection of papers on the state-of-the-art in the various social science disciplines.

4. John Kenneth Galbraith, *The New Industrial State* (Boston: Houghton Mifflin Co., 1967).

5. Oliver P. Williams, Harold Herman, Charles S. Liebman, and Thomas R. Dye, *Suburban Differences and Metropolitan Policies: A Philadelphia Story* (Philadelphia: University of Pennsylvania Press, 1965).

6. Elliott Sclar, "Aging and Residential Location," in *Community Planning for an Aging Society*, eds. M. Powell Lawton, Robert J. Newcomer, and Thomas O. Byerts (Stroudsberg, Penn.: Dowden, Hutchinson and Ross, 1976), pp. 266-281.

7. Martin Lowenthal, "The Social Economy in Urban Working Class Communities," in *The Social Economy of Cities*, ed. Rose Gappert (Beverly Hills, Calif.: Sage Publications, 1975), pp. 446-469.

8. K.H. Schaeffer and Elliott Sclar, *Access for All: Transportation and Urban Growth* (London: Penguin Books, 1975), ch. 7.

9. Elliott Sclar, "The Community Basis for Economic Development," in *Whatever Happened to Minority Economic Development*, ed. Samuel Doctors (Hinsdale, Ill.: Dryden Press, 1974), pp. 56-65.

10. See, for example, Peter B. Doeringer and Michael J. Piore, *Internal Labor Markets and Manpower Analysis* (Lexington, Mass.: Lexington Books, D.C. Heath and Co., 1971).

11. Walter Leutz, "Work and Aging: The Relevance of Marxian Labor Process Theory" (substantive paper, Brandeis University, 1978).

12. James H. Schulz, *Economics of Aging* (Belmont, Calif.: Wadsworth Publishing Co., 1976), ch. 2.

13. Almost 25 percent of all households where the head is over sixty-five had 1975 incomes of less than $5,000. This compares to less than 9 percent for households where the head was between twenty-five and sixty-five years of age in 1975. Source: "Income and Poverty Among the Elderly, 1975," *Statistical Reports on Older Americans 2*, Administration on Aging, April, 1977.

14. In 1976 the amount of such income was $3,000. According to the Bureau of Labor Statistics, a minimum level budget for a retired couple living in the Boston metropolitan area that year cost $5,172. Sources: Social Security Administration and the U.S., Department of Labor, Bureau of Labor Statistics Release no. 77-690.

15. Elliott Sclar, testimony before the U.S., House, Congress, Select Committee on Aging, 6 May 1977, on the subject of retirement age policies, Committee publication no. 95-95, pp. 70-78.

16. Schulz, *Economics of Aging*, ch. 6.

17. Suzanne G. Haynes, Anthony J. Michael, and Herman Tyroler, "Survival After Early and Normal Retirement," *Journal of Gerontology* 33(1978): 269-278.

18. We must, however, distinguish between those jobs which are onerous and from which retirement is viewed as a blessing and those which involve power and decision-making authority. It is generally loss of the latter that creates problems of adjustment. However, work status loss can cause serious problems even when the work in considered unpleasant. See, Gerda G. Fillenbaum and George L. Maddox, "Work After Retirement," *The Gerontologist* 14(1974):418-424 and Leutz, "Work and Aging."

19. J. Kevin Eckert, "Urban Renewal and Redevelopment: High Risk for the Marginally Subsistant Elderly," *The Gerontologist* 19(1979):496-502.

20. Bernice L. Neugarten, "Age Groups in American Society and the Rise of the Young-Old," *The Annals of the American Academy of Political and Social Science* 415(1974):187-198.

21. Earl C. Gottshalk, "As Some Sunbelt Sites Get Crowded, Retirees Head for the Country," *Wall Street Journal*, 13 November 1979, p. 1.

22. Alan Sagen, "Estimating the Costs of Diverting Patients from Nursing Homes to Home Care." (Presented at the Thirtieth Annual Meeting of the Gerontological Society, San Francisco, Calif., November, 1977).

# 4 Old Women: Problems, Potential, and Policy Implications

*Beth B. Hess*

The emergence of large numbers of elderly women is a rather recent phenomenon of advanced industrial societies. Even when it was obvious that old women composed a substantial majority of the older population in the United States, decades passed before some gerontologists made them the center of research and theoretical concern. A short history of the "woman question" in the Gerontological Society serves as a paradigm of the condition of older women in society in general.

## The Gerontological Society and the Woman Question

As a latter day feminist and recycled homemaker myself, I was—am—perhaps overly sensitive to feminist issues in academe. Having achieved a minor success in gerontology and being fortunate enough to have made friends among highly respected female colleagues, I began asking such questions as, "Why are there no major symposia on older women at the Gerontological Society meetings?" and "Why is there no women's caucus in the Gerontological Society to support younger women faculty?" The answer to the latter was that women had long held high office in the Gerontological Society and were well represented in universities with gerontological programs. As for the former question, most of those with whom I spoke did not perceive that older women's interests were being overlooked, an attitude based on the assumption that all research on aging must automatically incorporate elderly females.

However, it became clear to me and a few others that, as the field began to receive enormous funds from federal and state sources and as gerontological courses and programs and centers were mushrooming, gerontology was now big academic business. Hence it was attracting a different class of academics—younger, achievement-oriented males—who were slowly replacing women in the hierarchy. It was increasingly obvious that women had done so well in the field only because it was a low-status specialty before the Older Americans Act, and it remained so as long as it was underfunded, until the 1970s. Elsewhere my colleague, Elizabeth Markson, and I have suggested that this state of affairs illustrates the sociological concept of a "halo effect" whereby practitioners assume the social status of their clients. Thus internists are more highly evaluated than pediatricians, corporate attorneys than divorce specialists, and sociologists of work over those who study family or sex roles.

As for the relative neglect of the study of older women, many doubters were persuaded by a symposium on "Women as They Age" at the 1975 Gerontological Society meeting. The room was packed, indeed, had to be changed to accommodate all those wishing to hear some breakthrough material. The disappointment at the absence of such material was enough that I decided to convene a women's caucus in my hotel room. The aim was to put together an entire program on aging women for the following year, and several dozen people agreed to assist the effort. It was, however, left to me to keep the whole idea going, and over the course of the following year one after another of the women who had agreed to write papers found that they were unable to do so. My request for a symposium was turned down by the program committee, and I ran out of steam soon thereafter.

That was in 1975, the year that also saw publication of two scathing critiques of gerontology written by women sociologists: Diane Beeson in *Social Problems*, and Arlie Hochschild in *American Sociological Review*. Their theses were more sophisticated than my tentative criticisms, especially with regard to the research agenda and dominant theories, both clearly framed from a male perspective. Yet there was no ground swell at the 1976 meetings, although more sessions were devoted to aging women than at previous meetings. So the Women's Caucus died aborning. But the 1977 Gerontological Society meeting was a different case. Unknown to me, several women were establishing an organization named the National Action Forum for Old Women NAFOW. They tacked up hand-lettered signs inviting interested parties to an informal discussion of the need for such a body. Dozens came, and NAFOW is now a viable (though undernourished) organization. Wisely, the founders asked the top two dozen gerontologists to serve on an Advisory Board (and most agreed). With this support they proceeded to develop a national network called FORUM.

The other galvanizing feature of the 1977 meeting was the reaffirmation by the Gerontological Society Council of plans to meet in 1978 in New Orleans, Louisiana, a state that had not ratified the Equal Rights Amendment. Opposition to this decision was led by another group of women, several of whom were officers of the society. We petitioned the council to reconsider again, began a petition campaign, and talked darkly of boycotting New Orleans. The infighting at this point was apparently quite bloody for a professional association, with one of the male council members muttering about "hysterical women." I was asked not to continue to "make trouble," and dire predictions about the outcome of "politicizing a scientific society" were directed at "the crazies." An attempt to mollify us by agreeing to make the older women the focus of the 1978 meeting, failed to dampen our ardor. Soon after the 1977 meetings ended the council met twice again, ultimately deciding to hold the meetings in Dallas, Texas, a ratified state.

The meetings were held in Dallas and the promise to focus on older women was kept, although the Gerontological Society lost money on the annual meeting

for the first time. The costs of changing the meeting place and a lowered attendance were cited as primary reasons, although one suspects that attendance
would have been even lower in New Orleans. But the point was clearly made:
the concerns of older women should be central to those who study the aged.
As a latent consequence the position of women in the field was reinforced. It
will become clear in the remainder of this chapter why feminist issues are of
crucial significance in the lives of older women, though very few of them are
sympathetic to, much less active participants in, the Women's Movement.

## Why Should Older Women Be Considered a Special Case?

In a very real sense it is older men and not women who should be considered
the special case.[1] Not only do women sixty-five and over outnumber men in
the same age group—over 13.5 million to almost 9.5 million—but this differential
will increase through the remainder of this century. In the year 2000, given
current age-specific death rates, there will be 18.5 million older women compared to 12 million men. In other words what is today a difference of 4 million
will become 6.5 million over the next two decades, with much of this coming
at the oldest categories. Compared with males, the female population will be
older, particularly at age eighty and over.

As might be surmised from these data, the ratio of women to men will
continue to increase (with the exception of sixty-five- to sixty-nine- year-
olds) between 1977 and 2000. Looking at the trends in this century:

| *Ratio of Women to Men,* *Sixty-five and Over:* | *1900-2000* |
|---|---|
| 1900 | 98/100 |
| 1930 | 100/100 |
| 1970 | 139/100 |
| 2000 | 154/100 |

Source: U.S., Department of Health, Education and Welfare,
*Facts About Older Americans*, 1976.

There are a number of arguments advanced to explain the difference between male and female survival rates in this century. One of the most popular
is that the type of work done by men places them at risk of heart attacks, a
leading cause of death for males, and other cerebrovascular accidents. However,
there is evidence that females are by nature long-lived and that this has been
masked through human history by the morbidity and mortality risks of

childbearing and by a tendency for women and female children to absorb most of the effects of famine and malnutrition.[2]

Thus, only in this century have females survived childhood and adulthood in large numbers. Even now, as life styles of men and women are converging in terms of alcohol consumption, cigarette smoking, and stressful occupations (although sweatshops and mills cannot have been salubrious environments), female mortality rates continue to decline relative to males.

Another measure of differential survival is the average number of years at birth that an individual can expect to live, that is, *life expectancy*. The vital statistics data for the United States in this century are striking: at birth in 1900, white males could expect to live 48.2 years, nonwhite males, 32.5 years; by 1976, white males at birth could expect to live 69.7 years and nonwhites 64.1 years. Comparable figures for females, however, show more dramatic gains, from 51.1 years in 1900 to 77.3 years in 1976 for whites, and from 35.0 to 72.6 years for nonwhites.

The world of the aged is increasingly a society of old women. This realization alone should have encouraged long ago an exploration of what has been dubbed "the double whammy" of being old and female in America today.[3]

### Sociocultural Context: Attitudes Toward Old People

*Agism* is a set of attitudes and behaviors toward the elderly that are negative and discriminatory. The case for agism is often made with more passion than data, and there is much evidence that old people themselves do not buy the stereotype for themselves.[4]

In general, American attitudes toward aging and old people are not positive; youthfulness is the preferred condition.[5] The research findings, mostly from psychology on small samples with a large number of variables, are difficult to categorize since each study is slightly different from the others. From several recent attempts to test differences by sex in images of the elderly come the following:

Evaluation of stimulus concepts was increasingly negative with age of stimulus, with females perceived as less autonomous and effective up to age seventy-five. But female stimulus figures were more personally acceptable at all ages. The female subjects in the study were less sex differentiating in their responses than were male subjects.[6]

Stimulus pictures of females were assigned by subjects to older age categories and perceived to get older sooner than male stimulus figures. The oldest subjects were not as sex biased as the younger ones, and females in general were more tolerant than males of age differences.[7]

Subjects rated an older female stimulus figure more favorably than a younger one, especially when behavior did not correspond to stereotypical expectations.[8]

And so it goes; each study slightly more complex than the last, with different subjects, stimuli, and statistical techniques. Apparently very old females do not arouse strong feelings and can be looked upon rather indulgently. Also as the sex-role socialization literature suggests, female test-takers are softer in their judgments than are males.

Nor is there much agreement on the effects of these attitudes or stereotypes. The connections between self-identification as old, attitudes toward old people in general, and self-esteem are not at all clear, although there are statistical correlations that differ by sex.[9] Some argue that self-esteem is antecedent to age-identification and attitudes toward the elderly,[10] while the logic of the "looking-glass self" would suggest that self-esteem is affected by negative attitudes in others.

*The Double Standard of Aging*

If agism is hard to pin down, sexism is not. No laboratory experiments are required to verify denigration of females at ages up to seventy-five even if the very old and frail are to be excepted. Some of the viciousness of these evaluations, however, do seem mitigated when the target is an old woman. A study of 100 jokes about the aged shows that while old women are almost the exclusive butts of jokes about lying about their age and undesirable aspects of aging, males alone are thought to suffer sexual and physical decline, and all but a few of the positive themes are accorded male subjects.[11]

Why should women be so fearful of betraying their true age, and men of losing potency? Because beauty is the primary value by which women are judged in our society, while strength and vigor are the men's claim to worth. This means that each sex will age according to a different timetable, women earlier than men. The double standard of aging, so beautifully demonstrated in the joke study,[12] is also reflected in our immediate reaction to the sight of an older woman escorted by a young male in contrast to an old man and young woman, and the relative frequency of each type of couple. Data on remarriage show that rates for men are, overall, three times those of women, but four times higher for widowed persons, that is, the older age categories.[13] Widowers are much more quickly introduced to potential partners than are widowed or divorced women as young as forty-five or fifty. The older man is still a "good catch" because he is assumed to be sexually potent and is financially and socially superior to most older women. The elderly female, however, has irrevocably lost those qualities that make her catch-worthy—fertility and the beauty that resides in youthfulness. Making it on personality alone has never been easy for women.

All of these reasons may account for a benign neglect of older women in the popular culture. Studies of print advertisements as well as of children's books and other literature clearly document the relative absence of old women, and their passive dependent traits when portrayed (a fate that could be considered preferable to that of younger females in advertisements and books).[14] [15]


## The Wicked Witch of the West

Something very serious is happening. We laugh at that which we fear and ignore what would upset us to confront. The trivialization of women, their reduction to body parts when young and dismissal as persons when old, masks something more disturbing than the fact that young females are perceived as sexy and older ones are not.

The aging woman also evokes fear. That is what the ridicule is all about. Those who were children in the 1930s and 1940s will remember Maggie and Jiggs; she was of the rolling-pin type, prototypical nag, queen of a procession of battle-axes. There was also Philip Wylie's best selling *A Generation of Vipers*, the anti-mom diatribe that spawned a literary generation of hate-women novels, including the work of Norman Mailer and culminating in Philip Roth's portrait of Mother Portnoy. Castrating mothers, greedy wives who withhold sex, and their own problems with bowel movements are the dominant themes of borscht-belt comedians.

Well, what else can a man laugh at? And it is also the case that women join the laughter. But Livson suggests deeper currents: "The idealization of the young woman no less than the devaluation of the old is born of a deep-seated ambivalence toward women which lurks in the unconscious of the culture."[16] The image of a mother goddess is rooted, suggests Livson, in our earliest experience as helpless infants, but only the male child must resent his dependence and define himself as other than the omnipotent nurturer. Thus is bred the need to dominate women; younger ones are things without power, but the older ones evoke the primal fear of losing one's identity in that amorphous mass of love. The adult male, therefore, has to separate his fear of women from his attraction to them sexually. This can be accomplished through the denigration of old women and the sexual objectification of young ones. Livson looks to the changes in self-esteem of all women, as a consequence of the Women's Movement, to enhance the images of older women, and also to whatever family patterns will decrease the matriarchal atmosphere of infancy and childhood.

It must be added here that mother and daughter relationships are not as unproblematic as the psychological literature has long assumed. A recent spate of academic and popular work on the subject has opened up this previously tabooed area.[17] Boys and girls, then, find themselves in her thrall, and ever after must deal with the fear of obliteration she evokes. Here is another root of the "symbolic annihilation" of women found in the media by Tuchman.[18] Who are these anxiety-producing creatures, and what shape will they take in the future?

### Old Women Today

I use the term *old women* rather than *older women* since the latter has become rather amorphous, often a euphemism. It sounds less frightening than "old" and frequently is extended to cover all those over age forty. The recent intense interest in midlife women has produced a great deal of material relevant to understanding women over age sixty, and two excellent bibliographies.[19] As the girl is mother to the woman, so today's midlife women are the aged of tomorrow. Throughout this chapter it must be borne in mind that the category of sixty-five and over includes several disparate subgroups. Women in their sixties and early seventies are very different from those eighty and over. Measurements that are averages for the entire range overestimate the resources of the very old and underestimate those of women at the younger range. Subgroups will be distinguished wherever the data allow.

### Nativity

In 1920 over 13 percent (almost all of whom are now sixty-five and over) were foreign born, a figure that is well under 5 percent today. Moreover, a majority of today's elderly women were the children of parents both of whom were foreign born. This suggests that from their own experience or early socialization in the family these women have been exposed to traditional values and expectations regarding the proper role of kin in caring for the aged. There is some evidence that old people with extended expectations of their offspring are often disappointed since the children's performance will invariably fall short.[20] While such attitudes need not be associated with ethnicity, among the urban widows studied by Lopata those with old-country values were more dissatisfied with their children's behavior toward them and were less able to recover from their husband's death than were somewhat younger and presumably more modern widows.[21]

### Marital Status and Living Arrangements

As the data on life expectancy indicates, women outlive men. If most men marry women younger than themselves, then wives will certainly outlive their husbands. So it is that the great majority of elderly women spend their last years as widows. Although the current trend is toward smaller age differences in a first marriage, from four years in 1900 to two years in 1974,[22] and although male life expectancy has also increased, this simply means that today's wives will become widowed at later ages than did their mothers but will remain widowed for an equal or longer period. In 1976 at ages sixty-five to sixty-nine almost half of elderly women were living with their husbands, as were almost four-fifths of men in that age range. For the age range seventy-four to seventy-nine, three-quarters of men were living with their wives, but less than one-third of women this age were living with a spouse. The data for 1984 are only marginally different, the percentages for living with spouse for both sexes increasing slightly. The only significant change in living arrangements expected in the near future is a continuation of the trend of the past decade toward an increase in older women living alone rather than as a residual category, typically in the home of a daughter.

The evidence from survey data is that this is the preferred pattern for old women and their offspring, but apparently not until quite recently have they been able to realize this preference. Undoubtedly, improved income maintenance through the extension of social security benefits is a major factor, as is the removal, with the advent of Medicare, of the threat of insolvency due to medical expenses.

A small fraction—less than 1 percent of all unmarried adults sixty-five and over-live with an unrelated person of the opposite sex.[23] Households in which the male was sixty-five and over comprised about 9 percent of all unmarried couple households in the United States in 1977.

Even though the proportion of female widows sixty to seventy-five is expected to decline, the percentage of women sixty-five and over who are divorced will increase substantially in the future: from 12 percent in 1975 to 22 percent in 2000, with higher percentages the lower the age. Not all widowed or divorced women will be unmarried at sixty-five or over, but the remarriage data strongly suggest that most who are not remarried by this age will remain without a spouse, though not necessarily without a partner.

## Education

White men and women entering old age (sixty to sixty-four) are getting, and will continue to get, increasingly more college education than their predecessors. It is predicted that by the year 2000 these white men will get proportionately more college education than white women.[24] However, these predictions do not take into account the large numbers of mature women returning to colleges in the 1970s to complete their education. Also, for the first time, the percentage of female high-school graduates going on to postsecondary institutions was

larger than that for males in 1977-1978.[25] Current projections probably underestimate the proportion of older women in 2000 who will have some college
education.[26] Education is an important indicator of well-being in old age for
two reasons: for men it has often been associated with occupational placement
and hence income, and for both men and women education is assumed to
enhance abilities to cope with the exigencies of modern life. Women who are
sixty-five and over today are educationally disadvantaged compared to subsequent cohorts (although up to 1970 most old women have had more formal
education than have old men). If we were to examine the occupational and
income returns from years of school completed, it would be clear that men in
general, probably at each educational level, are more amply rewarded than
women. Nonetheless education is an important variable in the lives of old
women. In the Texas Study on Aging, Blau reports that education was the
single most powerful corelate of well-being among elderly women,[27] and Lopata
concludes that education was of great importance in a woman's ability to
reformulate an identity following widowhood.[28]

   Combined with ethnic status and the probability of socialization to traditional expectations, the limited educational attainment of many old women
today seems to encourage a passive, dependent response to the physical and
social insults of aging.

*Labor-force Participation*

Contrary to much idealized thinking about the good old days when women
stayed home, raised broods, and produced a cornucopia of homemade goodies,
between two-fifths and one-half of women who are sixty-five and over today
were in the labor force during their middle age: in 1960, 49.3 percent of women
between the ages of forty-five and fifty-four were in the labor force, and in
1970 when these women were fifty-five to sixty-four, participation rates were
a robust 42.5 percent.[29] Today at age sixty-five less than 8 percent are working for pay.

   Up until the 1970s it was women of lower economic status who were most
likely to be employed. From 1970 on the increase in female labor-force participation has been largely among women whose education and family income ranks
them in the middle class. Those who are sixty-five and over today must have
entered the labor market at fairly low levels, earned accordingly, and had erratic
patterns of participation. As a consequence not only were incomes from work
low, but the necessary quarters for coverage under social security, and many
were in employment not covered until recent decades, was often not attained.
As low-skilled and low-paying as their employment may be, older female
workers show great attachment to the labor force, frequently reluctant to leave
(often only to keep retired husbands company), and often enjoying a morale

advantage over those who are not working for pay.[30] Their work, however, does not typically bring the material rewards essential to a comfortable old age.

*Income*

Most old women are dependent on social security benefits as their sole source of income, not necessarily the benefits accrued from their own employment but the survivor's benefits derived from their husband's working life, and the additional benefits some receive as spouses of a current recipient. Indeed for most who have worked, the half of a retired husband's benefit to which a wife is entitled is greater than the amount they can expect from their own social security account. No credit is given for unpaid work in the home other than the widow's mite and the dependent's stipend. Old women are far more likely than not to be "unrelated individuals,"[31] and the incidence of poverty among them is quite high. Almost 30 percent of widows sixty-five and over in 1976 had incomes below the poverty line of $2,722 for an unrelated elderly female (the comparable sum for an unrelated male sixty-five and over is $2,758). The wonder is that so many are still able to maintain the independent residence and autonomy that they desire.

*Physical and Mental Health*

**Morbidity**: Although they outlive men, women of all ages have higher rates of illness, make more physician visits, and are hospitalized for more days than men. In part this may be due to differential sex-role socialization to the sick role and in part may represent differences in health status, but it may also account for women's longevity advantage. However, the fact that so many women live to such old ages means that disability and frailty increasingly characterize their last days. Nursing homes are largely occupied by women in their eighties and nineties who have several chronic conditions rendering self-care impossible. The nursing-home problem is one especially affecting women, which might account for much of the neglect in the homes and among public officials.

Before they themselves become objects of care, most old women have attended the terminal illness of their husband. Over four-fifths of Lopata's widows had cared for a dying husband at home.[32] Caring for a disabled husband, however, is not without its toll in isolation, hardship, and role overload.[33] Turner notes that the increased power of the wife vis-à-vis a disabled husband does not extend outside the home and even ties her to the home more securely than before.[34]

**Personality and Mental Health**: Undoubtedly the most interesting finding to come out of the psychological literature on old age is that which reports the personality changes at midlife and after, whereby aging men "move from active to passive mastery" and aging women the reverse.[35] In general, older men are more likely than younger ones to display expressive personality traits, and older women compared with younger ones to evince the masculine traits of dominance and assertiveness. Just what this means is a subject of lively debate.

Following Gutmann, some believe that the demands of motherhood for women and occupational success for men require a masking of sex-inappropriate traits, so that only when these major tasks are essentially completed can individuals relax inhibitions and display cross-sex-typed personality tendencies.[36] Gutmann refers to a "normal unisex" of later life, but Turner points out that the woman's increasing assertiveness is still not approved by others for conduct outside the home, making her even less comfortable with herself in some ways.[37] Huyck draws attention to the higher rates of hospitalization for depression among women compared to men in late middle age but allows that *androgyny*, the mixture of feminine and masculine traits, could be a healthier state for women beyond the years of child-rearing than is the highly feminized personality of midlife women facing the empty nest.[38] It is these latter to whom Bart refers in her classic essay "Portnoy's Mother's Complaint": the "perfect," sacrificing, "Jewish Mother"—and you don't have to be Jewish to be one, only overinvolved in your children's lives—who is disproportionately represented among hospitalized depressives.[39] Gove and Tudor also relate the high incidence of mental illness among adult women to the psychological constraints of the female sex role.[40]

For those who do not succumb to depression or psychosomatic illness during the menopause or when their children leave home, the personality changes of later life are associated with positive levels of self-esteem. Turner suggests that because male-female differences on personality measures are less extreme in old age than at previous life stages, differences in self-esteem will also be minimized.[41] If women recognize in themselves highly valued male-linked traits, they should feel better about themselves. In general men and women of any age who display psychological androgyny are also more adaptable when situations require non-sex-types responses.[42] This is certainly a requirement of old age, especially for women who are widowed.

Troll and Turner add a corrective caveat to these speculations by noting that the phrase "normal unisex" is inaccurate since both sexes' personalities remain composed predominately of same-sex traits; nor is it any more precise to speak of "role convergence" since the repertoire of sex-role behaviors remain quite distinct.[43] What are being discussed, say Troll and Turner, are intrapsychic changes with concomitant consequences in self-esteem, although it is not clear whether this is a developmental imperative as Gutmann concludes, or a personality change that can vary by cohort experience.

If mental health can be assessed using suicide rate as a rough index, it is significant that for white females, suicide rates peak at midlife—forty-five to fifty-four—while those of white males continue to increase with age.[44] It is a sad commentary on our society that the suicide rates for nonwhites peak for both men and women between ages twenty-five to thirty-four.

Yet there is much social survey data to support the thesis that postmeno-pausal and postparental couples have higher levels of morale, life satisfaction, or whatever is being measured as a positive trait than do individuals and couples in the years immediately preceding the empty nest. Miller simply suggests that this is due to the presence of teenagers in the home and attendant stress.[45]

For whatever reasons, old women are not overly burdened by negative self-evaluation although the attitudes of others toward them may be ambivalent in the extreme. Despite losses, material and social, increasing frailty and loneli-ness, old women are a hardy breed, and the qualities associated with adapt-ability, independence, and successful coping will be more characteristic of incoming cohorts of old women compared to those now sixty-five and over.

**The New Old Woman**

In most of the areas discussed, many of which place old women today at some disadvantage in dealing with social systems outside the family and neighbor-hood—traditional upbringing, low education, fitful and ill-paid employment, hostility and indifference from others—incoming cohorts of elderly women will differ significantly. Table 4-1 is taken from Neugarten and Brown-Rezanka and summarizes demographic characteristics of American women in 1975.[46]

Although the youngest cohort—group C women between twenty-five and thirty in 1975—has not completed either its fertility or employment history, it is clear that, like group B, members will come to old age with a very different set of life experiences than group A who are today's sixty-five to seventy-year-olds. Table 4-1 well illustrates the necessity of looking at cohort data in histor-ical context. For example, the effects of the Depression are clearly evident in the late marriage, delayed births, and relative childlessness of the oldest group. The Depression babies (group B) were almost twice as likely as their mothers' generation to come from small families; they also married earlier and bore more children at younger ages. Educational attainment, labor-force participation, and entry into professional jobs all show a secular increase from the oldest cohort to the youngest. Note also that by group C's advent almost all cohort members are the offspring of native-born parents and that only 15 percent will have witnessed the death of a parent or sibling by age fifteen. Over half of the women who are sixty-five to seventy today had experienced such a death before their fifteenth birthday.

The combination of secular trend and peculiar cohort history is most strikingly evidenced in the marriage and family data. The low birth rates of young women today approximate that of their grandmothers' rather than their mothers' generation, though for different reasons. What is clear is that

**Table 4-1**
**Social Characteristics of American Women in 1975**

|  | Group A Ages 60 to 65 | Group B Ages 40 to 45 | Group C Ages 25 to 30 |
|---|---|---|---|
| Total number[a] | 4,983 | 5,735 | 8,909 |
| Average life expectancy at birth | 55 | 63 | 70 |
| **Education** | | | |
| Percent completed high school | 53 | 72 | 84 |
| Percent one or more years of college | 17 | 23 | 38 |
| Percent graduated from college | 8 | 11 | 20 |
| **Labor force participation** | | | |
| Percent in labor force at present | 33 | 57 | 57 |
| Percent in professional and technical jobs | 12 | 17 | 25 |
| **Early family experience[b]** | | | |
| Percent whose parents both born in United States | 46 | 85 | 94 |
| Percent with one or no sibling | 18 | 30 | 20 |
| Percent to age 15 in families with no deaths of parents or siblings | 45 | 71 | 85 |
| **Marriage and family** | | | |
| Percent first married by age 20 | 37 | 50 | 46 |
| Percent single at age 25 to 29 | 23 | 10 | 15 |
| Percent divorced by age 35 to 39[c] | 12 | 18 | (4) |
| Percent first marriage ended (or predicted to end) in divorce | 16 | 26 | 38 |
| For married women | | | |
| Average number of births by age 27 | 1.1 | 2 | 1.4 |
| Total number of births per woman | 2.5 | 3.2 | 1.5[d] |
| Percent first birth within 7 months of marriage | 11 | 14 | 23 |
| Percent childless at age 25 to 29 | 30 | 13 | 21 |

Source: Bernice L. Neugarten and Lorill Brown-Rezanka, "A Midlife Woman in the 1980's," in *Women and Midlife-Security and Fulfillment*, Select Committee on Aging, U.S. House of Representatives (Washington, D.C.: Government Printing Office, 1978), p. 35. Data are taken from various reports of the U.S. Bureau of the Census and the Bureau of Labor Statistics.

[a]As of 1 July 1977. Parallel numbers of men are 4,380, 5,465, and 8,837.

[b]Data on early family experience are for white native-born, both sexes combined. For group C, data are for persons born in 1950. See Peter Uhlenberg, "Changing Configurations of the Life Course," a paper prepared for the Conference on the Family-Life Course in Historical Perspective, Williams College, July 1975.

[c]Seventeen percent of this group have already been divorced by age 25 to 29.

[d]This group is still in their childbearing years; their total birthrate will be higher.

each cohort will come to old age with a very different set of family resources. Group B, for example, will have more children but fewer siblings than A or C. Group C will have few children and a lowered probability of still being married but a longer life span. In general there is a negative association between number of offspring and the probability of a woman's becoming institutionalized in old age.[47] But group C women will have other characteristics that should enhance independent living: education, employment, and the prior experience of living alone. Group B women will have the advantages of large numbers of surviving children, of education and employment gains, and a relatively high probability of an intact marriage.

The society in which these women are embedded has changed, too. The two younger cohorts have been affected, whether acknowledged or not, by the Women's Movement. Group B women are returning to employment and school in record numbers, both absolutely and relative to other age groups. It may be too much to claim for the movement, yet, that major changes have taken place in attitudes toward women, but I believe that very few American women can have lived through the past decade without their sense of self having been touched by the feminist critique. Some will have been reinforced in their adherence to traditional sex roles, and others more or less changed by their encounter with the Women's Movement, but none has emerged without thinking about it.

My expectation is that the "new" old woman will bring a number of strengths to her later years: the abilities needed to cope with education, work experience, and adequate retirement incomes; the inner resources nurtured over a lifetime of self-respect; egalitarian relationships with men and other women; and the years of singleness before, between, and after marriage. However new the old women of the future, their lives will be ultimately shaped by their being the "second sex."

## Policy Implications

From all the foregoing it is clear that policies in both the short and long run must deal with the position of women as a whole, the special problems of the very old and frail (now and in the future when women's lives will extend to advanced ages), nonwhites who are especially deprived at all ages, working women, and those who will have minimal family supports. The list could go on since the older population is composed of many subgroups, and incoming cohorts will differ greatly from those now old and from one another.

Beginning with the broader perspective first, there are three major public policy thrusts that undergird a comprehensive program for America's elderly, the majority of whom are women.

*Income Maintenance*

Recent changes in the Social Security Act have pegged benefits to the cost of living, but large numbers of old women are attempting to support themselves on consistently meager benefits—less than $300 monthly. The report of the Task Force on Women and Social Security for the Special Committee on Aging of the U.S. Senate examines many ways in which current regulations penalize the homemaker and working woman.[48] Several of their recommendations were incorporated in the amendments of 1977, such as reducing from twenty to ten the number of years a widowed or divorced wife had to be married in order to be entitled to benefits from that marriage, and ending the reduction of benefits to those who remarry after age sixty. The major questions of social security credits for homemaking and inequities in dual-worker benefits were not addressed.

For the moment, policy makers have chosen to continue to fine-tune the existing social security system with its fiction of social insurance rather than tackle the crucial issue of income flow through the life course and redistributive equity. Nor is there much sentiment in the nation at large for such socialistic policies, but the longer periods of postemployment of the elderly, the continued high unemployment of some subgroups, and the nagging incidence of poverty in America will keep these issues on the political agenda. That income adequacy should be regarded as an entitlement rather than a reward for hard work is still quite alien to a nation imbued with the Puritan work ethic. There are changes occurring that could lead to a reassessment of income policies, among which the needs of an aging population are a salient factor.

*Health Care*

The 1965 Medicare and Medicaid legislation established a program of health insurance for the aged and the poor that has removed from the elderly and their families the fear that their life's savings would be depleted by the common chronic ailments of old age. These programs were fiercely opposed by the medical and hospital establishments that now profit so handsomely from them. An older person spends several hundred of dollars each year on medical costs not covered by Medicare: prosthetic devices such as canes, glasses, hearing aids; prescriptions; the first $60 of most doctor visits; the first $124 of a hospital stay; other daily hospital charges after a specified time; and most home-care costs. Additionally, the premiums paid by insurees have increased steadily.

The Medicare and Medicaid experiences are sobering to those who contemplate comprehensive national health insurance. The costs have exceeded expectations, fraud abounds (though rarely on the part of patients), and institutionalization is no more humane than ever. Nonetheless the challenge of constructing a viable and equitable health delivery system cannot be evaded long. One consequence is likely to be improved health status of incoming cohorts of elderly, from better life long care and earlier treatment of eventually debilitating chronic conditions.

## *The Equal Rights Amendment*

Although the application of the Equal Rights Amendment to old women may not be immediately apparent, any legislation that enhances the status of women will lessen negative stereotypes that affect the self-image and treatment of females at all ages.

## Short-term Policy Recommendations

For the *institutionalized* abuses are prevalent among proprietary homes as well as state hospitals. We can demand more rigorous surveillance and ombuds programs, but the essential nature of total institutions remains. Perhaps the best that can be expected are policies that encourage the operation of nursing homes by nonprofit charitable and religious associations.

For the *frail and very old* recommendations are made for legal assistance, especially in case of commitment proceedings.

For those requiring *home care*, third-party reimbursement programs should be extended to cover homemaking and health-aide visits and provision of meals.

For the *families* that choose to care for an elderly relative in their home, respite services, reimbursements for expenses, and a stipend for the provision of services and shelter should be provided. Congresswoman Millicent Fenwick is sponsoring legislation that allots an old person a fixed sum to "purchase" home care, including that provided by relatives.

For *working women* approaching retirement there should be preretirement counseling programs that concentrate on the special problems of women who will likely spend many years in one-person households. Early advisement on money management would be most beneficial.

Along with these improvements of the social security program must come major changes in the current private pension systems. In 1975 only 2 percent of widows of private pension recipients were receiving any survivor benefits. Most private plans did not offer a survivor option, and very few workers chose to take the option when it was offered. Recently enacted federal regulations, ERISA, will make it easier, but not mandatory, for workers to cover their dependents.[49]

For *homemakers* there should be coverage under social security in recognition of the contribution that such unpaid work makes to the well-being of families. In this fashion wives will be symbolically recognized as equal partners in a marriage and materially aided in old age whether still married or not. Passage of state Displaced Homemaker bills will assist the divorced and widowed who are not old enough to collect social security.

For *midlife women*, assistance in job training and placement, education grants, counseling and guidance facilities, and support for self-help groups should be made available. In other words, policies that encourage the reentry of women into the world outside the home and offer support for role changes in the transition period will also add to the ability to cope in old age.

*Legislation against age and sex discrimination* in housing, credit, employment, and participation in public programs such as CETA is essential to the ability of older women to maintain their independence.

Provision of *alternate living arrangements* for groups of older women who wish to share a residence should be made. This requires variances in zoning ordinances that forbid unrelated individuals to live together. Public housing funds could also be used to provide a spectrum of living facilities from fully independent apartments to congregate quarters, offering gradations of health and homemaking services.

## Conclusions

With few exceptions these long- and short-term policy implications involve programs that will maintain an old woman in the community, enhance her well-being, provide options, and prevent dependency. Economic security is paramount, health care crucial, independence essential.

What do older women bring to their later years? Survivability, experience, and guts. Even the country-bred, unsophisticated, lonely widows interviewed by Lopata had a certain courage and dignity that permitted them to adapt to the changed conditions of their lives.[50] Stephens reports on the occupants of single occupancy rooms (S.R.O.S) in the inner city, women with minimal social and material resources who guard their autonomy from all intrusions.[51] A study of *shopping-bag ladies*, solitary wanderers of the urban night, similarly reveals a tenacious, if often deluded, self-sufficiency.[52]

There are many who do not hold out. Mental hospitals and nursing homes are full of very old and ill women. Some never recover from the role losses of middle age; having been socialized to a life of selfless devotion to others, they are bereft when those others leave. But the dominant pattern today is of searching, vital women who seek out new roles as volunteers, workers, students, and grand-mothers. Public policy, then, must have two foci: the dependent and the independent. Programs that encourage the latter should eventually reduce the former.

These women have much to teach us. Their era may be at hand, for here is
the strength and courage of those who try many things, who diversify their
life's holdings, who are blazing the trail that, with luck, the rest of us shall follow.

## Notes

1. Diane Beeson, "Women in Studies of Aging: A Critique and a Suggestion," *Social Problems* 23(1975):52-59; Arlie R. Hochschild, "Disengagement
Theory: A Critique and a Proposal," *American Sociological Review* 40(1975):
553-569.

2. Beth B. Hess and Elizabeth W. Markson, *Aging and Old Age: An Introduction to Social Gerontology* (New York: Macmillan, 1980).

3. Carol Nowak, Jurgis Karuza, and Jesse Namikas, "Youth, Beauty and
the Midlife Woman: The Double Whammy Strikes Again" (Presented at the
Conference on Women at Midlife, Cornell University, Ithaca, N.Y., 1976).

4. Timothy H. Brubaker and Edward A. Powers, "The Stereotype of
'Old': A Review and Alternative Approach," *Journal of Gerontology* 31(1976):
441-447.

5. Ruth Bennett and J. Eckman, "Attitude Toward Aging: A Critical
Examination of Recent Literature and Implications for Research," in *The
Psychology of Adult Development and Aging*, eds. Carl Eisdorfer and M. Powell
Lawton (Washington, D.C.: American Psychological Association, 1973); Lillian
Troll and Carol Nowak, "How Old Are You? The Question of Age Bias," in
*Counseling Adults*, eds. Nancy Schlossberg and Alan Entine (Monterey, Calif.:
Brooks Cole, 1977).

6. Agnes N. O'Connell and Naomi G. Rotter, "The Influence of Stimulus
Age and Sex on Person Perception," *Journal of Gerontology* 34(1979):220-228.

7. Nathan Kogan, "A Study of Age Categorization," *Journal of Gerontology* 34(1979):358-367.

8. Walter H. Crockett, Allan N. Press, and Marilynn Osterkamp, "The
Effect of Deviations from Stereotyped Expectations Upon Attitudes Toward
Older Persons," *Journal of Gerontology* 34(1979):368-374.

9. Russell A. Ward, "The Impact of Subjective Age and Stigma on Older
Persons," *Journal of Gerontology* 32(1977):227-232.

10. Brubaker and Powers, "The Stereotype of 'Old'."

11. Joseph Richman, "The Foolishness and Wisdom of Age: Attitudes
Toward the Elderly as Reflected in Jokes," *The Gerontologist* 17(1977):
210-219.

12. Inge Bell, "Double Standard of Aging," *Trans-action/Society* 8(1970):
75-80; Susan Sontag, "The Double Standard of Aging," *Saturday Review*
23(1972):29.

13. U.S. Department of Health, Education and Welfare, *Remarriages: United States*, Vital and Health Statistics, series P-21, no. 25, (Rockville, Md.: Government Printing Office, 1973).

14. Carol Hollenshead and Berit Ingersoll, "Older Women: A Study or Print Advertisement" (Presented at the Annual Meeting of the Gerontological Society, Dallas, Texas, 1978).

15. Edward F. Ansello, "Old Age and Literature: A Developmental Analysis," *Educational Gerontology* 2(1977):211-366; Bennett and Eckman, *The Psychology of Adult Development and Aging*.

16. Compare, H.E. Lerner, "Early Origins of Envy and Devaluation of Women: Implications for Sex Role Stereotypes," *Bulletin of the Menninger Clinic* 38(1974):538-553; Florine Livson, "Cultural Faces of Eve: Images of Women" (Presented at American Psychological Association, San Francisco, Calif., 1977).

17. Nancy Chodorow, *The Reproduction of Mothering: Psychoanalysis and the Sociology of Gender* (Berkeley, Calif.: University of California Press, 1978); and Nancy Friday, *My Mother, Myself* (New York: Dell, 1978).

18. Gaye Tuchman, "Introduction," in *Hearth and Home: Images of Women in the Mass Media*, eds. Gaye Tuchman, Arlene Kaplan Daniels, and James Benet (New York: Oxford University Press, 1978).

19. Marilyn R. Block, Janice L. Davidson, Jean D. Grambs, and Katheryn E. Serock, *Unchartered Territory: Issues and Concerns of Women Over 40* (College Park, Md.: Center on Aging, University of Maryland, 1978); U.S. Congress, House Select Committee on Aging, *Women in Midlife—Security and Fulfillment* (Washington, D.C.: Government Printing Office, 1978).

20. Wayne C. Seelbach and William J. Sauer, "Filial Responsibility Expectations and Morale Among Aged Parents," *The Gerontologist* 17(1977): 492-499.

21. Helena Znaniecki Lopata, "Self-Identity in Marriage and Widowhood," *The Sociological Quarterly* 14(1973):407-418.

22. Harriet B. Presser, "Age Differences Between Spouses," *American Behavioral Scientist* 19(1975):190-205.

23. Paul C. Glick, "Perspectives on the Living Arrangements of the Elderly" (Presented at Gerontological Society Annual Meeting, San Francisco, Calif., 1977).

24. Peter Uhlenberg, "Changing Structure of the Older Population of the USA During the Twentieth Century," *The Gerontologist* 17(1977):197-202.

25. Bernice L. Neugarten and Lorill Brown-Rezanka, "A Midlife Woman in the 1980's" in *Women in Midlife—Security and Fulfillment*, U.S. Congress, House Select Committee on Aging (Washington, D.C.: Government Printing Office, 1978).

26. Uhlenberg, "Changing Structure of the Older Population."

27. Zena Smith Blau, Pamela P. Rogers, Richard C. Stephens, and George T. Oser, "School Bells and Work Whistles: Sounds that Echo a Better Life for Women in Later Years," in *Women in Midlife—Security and Fulfillment*, U.S. Congress, House Select Committee on Aging (Washington, D.C.: Government Printing Office, 1978).

28. Helena Znaniecki Lopata, *Widowhood in an American City* (Cambridge, Mass.: Schenckman, 1973).

29. U.S. Department of Commerce, *Statistical Abstract of the United States* (Washington, D.C.: U.S. Government Printing Office, 1978), p. 387.

30. Robert C. Atchley, *The Sociology of Retirement* (Cambridge, Mass.: Schenckman, 1976); Philip Jaslow, "Employment, Retirement and Morale Among Older Women," *Journal of Gerontology* 31(1976):212–218; Pauline K. Ragan, "Socialization for the Retirement Role: 'Cooling the Mark Out,'" (Presented at the American Psychological Association Annual Meeting, San Francisco, Calif., 1977).

31. Jacob S. Siegal, "Demographic Aspects of Aging and the Older Population in the United States," Current Population Reports, P-23, no. 59, (Washington, D.C.: Government Printing Office, 1976).

32. Lopata, *Widowhood in an American City*.

33. Alfred P. Fengler and Nancy Goodrich, "Wives of Elderly Disabled Men: The Hidden Patients," *The Gerontologist* 19(1979):175-183.

34. B. Turner, "Sex Roles Among Wives in Middle and Late Life" (Presented at the American Psychological Association, San Francisco, Calif., August, 1977). See also Lillian Troll and Carol Nowak, "How Old Are You? The Question of Age Bias," in *Counselling Adults*, eds. Nancy Schlossberg and Alan Entine (Monterey, Calif.: Brooks Cole, 1977); Lillian Troll, "Overcoming Age-Sex Discrimination," in *Women in Midlife—Security and Fulfillment*, U.S. Congress, House Select Committee on Aging (Washington, D.C.: Government Printing Office, 1978).

35. David Gutmann, "The Cross-Cultural Perspective: Notes Toward a Comparative Psychology of Aging," in *The Handbook of the Psychology of Aging*, eds. J.E. Birren and K.W. Schaie (New York: Van Nostrand Reinhart, 1977); David Chiriboga and Mayda Thurner, "Concept of Self," in *Four Stages of Life*, eds. Marjorie Fiske Lowenthal, Mayda Thurner, David Chiriboga, and Associates, (San Francisco: Jossey-Bass, 1975); Barbara F. Turner, "The Self Concepts of Older Women." (Presented at American Psychological Association, San Francisco, Calif., 1977).

36. David Gutmann, "The Hunger of Old Men," *Trans-action/Society* 9(1971):55-66.

37. Turner, "Sex Roles Among Wives."

38. M.H. Huyck, "Sex, Gender and Aging" (Presented at Annual Meeting of Gerontological Society, New York, 1976).

39. Pauline Bart, "Portnoy's Mother's Complaint," *Trans-action/Society* 8(1970):222-228.

40. Walter R. Gove and Jeanette Tudor, "Adult Sex Roles and Mental Illness," *American Journal of Sociology* 78(1973):812-835.

41. Turner, "Sex Roles Among Wives."

42. Sandra Bem, "Sex Role Adaptability: One Consequence of Psychological Androgeny," *Journal of Personality and Social Psychology* 31(1975): 634-643.

43. Troll and Nowak, "How Old Are You? The Question of Age Bias."

44. R.D. Patterson, R. Abrahams, and F. Baker, "Preventing Self-Destructive Behavior," *Geriatrics* 29(1974):115-118.

45. Brent C. Miller, "A Multivariate Developmental Model of Marital Satisfaction," *Journal of Marriage and the Family* 38(1976):643-657.

46. Neugarten and Brown-Rezanka, "Midlife Woman in the 1980's."

47. Beth J. Soldo and George C. Myers, "The Effects of Total Fertility on Living Arrangements Among Elderly Women" (Presented at Gerontological Society Annual Meeting, New York, 1976).

48. U.S., Congress, Senate, Special Committee on Aging, "Women and Social Security: Adapting to a New Era" (Washington, D.C.: Government Printing Office, October 1975).

49. F. Young and L. Young. *Everything You Should Know About Pension Plans.* (Bethesda, Md.: Bethesda Books, 1976).

50. Lopata, *Widowhood in an American City.*

51. Joyce Stephens, *Loners, Losers and Lovers: A Sociological Study of the Aged Tenants of a Slum Hotel* (Seattle: University of Washington Press, 1977).

52. Jennifer Hand, "Shopping Bag Ladies in Urban Areas," mimeographed (New School for Social Research, 1977).

# 5

# Ethnicity and Aging: Public Policy and Ethnic Differences in Aging and Old Age

*Allan R. Meyers*

Americans are ambivalent about ethnicity. On the one hand, we celebrate the diversity of our ethnic backgrounds while on the other we have often insisted that public policy be blind to the particular interests of ethnic, racial, or national groups. The past two decades' experience has shown that neither the strength of ethnic loyalties nor the magnitude of ethnic differences has declined to any appreciable degree. Accordingly there has been a renewed interest in ethnicity and ethnic differences, particularly as they affect social policy, including policy toward older adults.

With respect to old age and aging, policy interests have reflected one pre-eminent concern: to document, and ultimately to remedy, the disadvantages suffered by the aged members of ethnic minority groups. However, ethnicity is more than disadvantage, and social policy toward older people must reflect the strengths as well as the weaknesses that ethnicity entails.

## Ethnicity

There is a tendency to equate ethnicity with hardship and disability and regard ethnic minorities exclusively as deprived and disadvantaged groups. There is often a close association between ethnicity and disadvantage; many older people in the United States have been imprisoned, tortured, beaten, and made to suffer economic hardship and humiliation simply because of their association with one or another ethnic group. However, these experiences have usually been the consequences of ethnicity or of social reactions to ethnic groups; the essence of ethnicity and ethnic differences is more subtle and complex.

Recent studies of ethnicity by historians, psychologists, and social scientists indicate that the force of ethnic factors operates simultaneously on several planes.[1] At the broadest and most familiar level, ethnicity and ethnic differences are associated with such readily visible or audible characteristics as language, physical features, food preferences, and dress. Studies have confirmed the importance of these public and superficial signs of ethnicity as badges of identity, but they have also shown that they are nearly always associated with deeper and less evident ethnic traits.

These include a sentimental or ideological dimension which is often associated with a nation that may not necessarily be a political entity, a historical

or mythological episode, a race of people, or a church. This sentiment or ideology is, in turn, associated with a consciousness of group identity, a sense of
being similar to some people and, correspondingly, different from everyone
else. This is not to say that ethnic groups are monolithic nor that all members
have similar interests. On the contrary, studies have shown that they are often
characterized by intense factional rivalries and internal dissension. However,
ethnicity entails some level of intragroup solidarity and consensus, at least
vis-à-vis the community at large.

There is also a cultural dimension of ethnicity; that is, shared values and
norms of behavior which group members impose upon themselves, neighbors,
and families, and, insofar as possible, the outside world. These norms are often
reinforced by residential segregation, imposed or voluntary, in ethnic neighborhoods or quarters which restrict their daily encounters to other members of
the same ethnic group. And finally there are social and economic aspects of
ethnicity which express themselves as philanthropic organizations, mutual-aid
societies, and family and community networks of social support. By these
means, ethnic groups provide material and moral support to their members,
reinforcing group solidarity and supporting their members in a hostile or, at
best, indifferent world.

Ideally studies of ethnicity should include data at all of these levels: historical, psychological, social, and cultural. In fact they rarely do. Nevertheless
fragmentary data derived from a number of sources indicate the importance
of ethnicity, at all levels of expression, in the lives of older adults.

## Old Age and Ethnicity

Despite the renewed interest in ethnic Americans, there have been few studies
of American ethnicity and fewer still of older people in American ethnic communities.[2] However, the largest and most consistent sources of data—the U.S.
Census, vital record, and government documents—indicate that there are considerable numbers of ethnic older people, at least insofar as ethnicity reflects
three standard criteria: race, language, and place of birth.

According to the 1970 U.S. Census, of the 20.1 million persons sixty-five
and over,[3] about 1.7 million (8.6 percent) are nonwhite; of these, the vast
majority, about 90 percent, are black, and the others are either Asian-American,
native American, Hispanic, or "other," which is the total range of ethnic designa-
tions that the census allows.[4] As populations, nonwhite groups tend to be
younger than white people. While 10.3 percent of the white population is
sixty-five or older, 7.1 percent of the Asian-Americans, 7.0 percent of blacks,
and 5.7 percent of native Americans were in this age group. Hispanics have
the smallest proportion of old people (4.4 percent).

In all likelihood the nonwhite ethnic populations will ultimately follow
the same secular trend as other industrial populations—there will be an aging

of the populations and a corresponding increase in the proportions of older adults. However, since the proportionate size of the older population depends on a number of factors including mortality, fertility, and age-specific in- and out-migration, it is not possible to predict the timing or the magnitude of these changes at the present time.

Insofar as ethnicity is associated with foreign birth and immigration, older people are more likely than their younger counterparts to have been born outside of the United States.[5] The census shows that nearly 15 percent of the older population is foreign born, and another fifth were born in this country to parents who were foreign born. There is, of course, some overlap between the aged nonwhite population and the older population of foreign stock (the total of foreign born and first-generation native born). However, at the present time, the foreign-stock group is overwhelmingly white, with the greatest numbers having immigrated from Germany, Italy, Ireland, the United Kingdom, and the USSR.[6] Once again, this situation is likely to change. The great mass of white immigrants is now sixty-five years old or older. Barring some extraordinary circumstance, they will not be replaced by other European immigrants. In the future there will probably be a smaller immigrant population in general, composed largely of either Spanish-speaking or nonwhite individuals.

Neither the nonwhite nor the foreign-born aged are uniformly distributed throughout the country. Older blacks and Hispanic people are heavily concentrated in urban areas, especially innercities, as are older native Americans to an increasingly greater extent.[7] There are regional and local concentrations; for example, 34 percent of older Bostonians reported that they were of Irish ethnicity, while the greatest number of the older Chinese and Japanese Americans live on the West Coast.[8]

The census does not include data on language, except in reference to those who speak Spanish as a mother tongue. However, the Bureau of the Census has undertaken a special survey which indicates that 5 percent of the older population does not speak English; of these, 30 percent speak Spanish, 20 percent Italian, and the rest speak a number of other languages.[9]

These data do not necessarily mean that 95 percent of older people are fluent in English. The report does not specify the parameters of language facility, but the study apparently refers only to those who read or speak no English at all. Intensive local studies of older immigrants indicate that many are bilingual or polylingual. They speak or understand some English, but prefer to communicate in their native languages. Many others speak English but cannot read or read but cannot write.[10] Moreover, many older people, like many younger ones, speak variant forms or dialects of English or speak with regional or national accents, many of which are associated with ethnic groups.[11] Any of these factors may affect a person's ability to communicate with family, neighbors, or strangers, yet none of them can be adequately characterized by a simple straightforward answer on a survey questionnaire or a census form.

Census data and other national survey data are subject to a number of similar conceptual and methodological problems. For example, there has been consistent underreporting of nonwhite people. In the most recent census the national rate of underreporting for blacks and Spanish-speakers may have been as high as 7.7 percent.[12] There are no estimates of age-specific rates of under-reporting, but for a number of reasons—including living arrangements, residence, education, and income—older people may have been at particularly high risk of undercounts.[13]

The utility of census data is further limited by the response categories that the census forms allow.[14] For example, they say nothing about ethnic minorities that are too small to be of national prominence but which may be demographically or economically significant in a few locales. Nor do they provide data about ethnic groups with very small older populations but extraordinarily great health and social service needs. They do not account for such "stateless" peoples as Jews and Armenians, many of whom have come to the United States from a number of countries, including Germany, Italy, the United Kingdom, and the USSR. And census reports can offer no evidence of internal differences, schisms, and factions within each racial, linguistic, or national groups.

At a national or state level these limitations rarely have major impact, as most of the populations concerned are relatively small and localized. However, in those locales where there are heavy concentrations of minority groups with special needs and problems, the census's categories are too arbitrary and crude to guide policy.[15]

There has also been a number of intensive local-level studies of minority aged. In many cases these are anecdotal studies. However, they show the more subtle impact of ethnicity on the lives of older people in ways that census data never does.

These studies show, for example, that older people prefer to speak and read their native languages, even when they also read and speak English, and they express strong preferences for their traditional diets and for eating and offering food in traditional ways.[16] They affirm the importance of traditional values, which are often in conflict with those of their children and grandchildren, and they prefer the company of others of the same ethnic group.[17] They are likely to have been born and reared in ethnic neighborhoods in this country or abroad, and many continue to live in their ghettoes or barrios even after the neighborhoods' ethnic characters have changed.[18] Insofar as they participate in leisure activities, these activities are often sponsored by ethnic organizations, and insofar as they receive social services, these are often provided by ethnic groups.[19] These same groups sponsor clinics and hospitals where older people receive medical attention, and nursing homes and retirement homes where they may receive long-term care. This is not to romanticize the nature of ethnic communities. As Ishizuka found in her study of older Japanese-Americans in San Diego, even relatively small and homogeneous ethnic communities are characterized by distinct and often hostile factions defined by place of birth, place of education, and length of residence in the United States.[20]

These are, of course, composite data reflecting the experiences of different ethnic minorities in different locales. Meyerhoff has undertaken a detailed study of the participants in a small Jewish community center in Southern California which shows the articulation of all elements of one well-documented case.

The Center People were nearly all Jewish immigrants from central or eastern Europe who were in their eighties and older at the time of Meyerhoff's research. They were, in effect, a relic Jewish population; their neighborhood had previously had a large and active Jewish community, but since the early 1950s its social and ethnic character had changed. At the time of her study, the Jewish population had declined dramatically and with it the institutional network of synagogues, shops, and voluntary associations. By Meyerhoff's estimate, the community would disappear in another five or ten years.[21] However, the Center People still thought of themselves as part of a larger Jewish community and that community, in turn, provided them with a range of social services, including the center itself.

At the same time, Meyerhoff also found that the center was rife with factions, and interpersonal relations were often strained. In part these reflected personality conflict, but there were also long-standing differences based on politics, education, and social-class background.[22] However, these stresses and strains notwithstanding, there were certain ideals and principles that nearly all people affirmed and certain events and symbols with which they identified: Israel, Zionism, the Yiddish language, the horror of Nazi Germany.[23] To the center's members, the force of these symbols was more important than internal differences. Indeed, participation in these symbols was of the essence of being Jews.

For older black people, Japanese, Irish, Italians, or Armenians, there are other symbols—different triumphs and other tragedies. But in each case, the shared consciousness of these events, legendary or historical, and the persons associated with them are major defining features of their identification with an ethnic group. Although not all older people have had the same experiences, they have generally been exposed to similar sets of conditions and responded in similar ways.

## Multiple Jeopardy? Ethnicity and the Quality of Late Life

More than fifteen years ago the National Urban League described the "double jeopardy" of being old and black in America. According to their report, the effects of a lifetime of poverty, poor education, and racial discrimination compounded the biological and social effects of aging. Consequently, they argued, older black people suffer an extra measure of hardship and disability that is directly attributable to their race.[24]

Since that time the concept of multiple jeopardies has been applied to the experiences of other minority elderly, who, like black Americans, face added disadvantages in old age.[25] The expression is to some extent misleading. Multiple jeopardy refers only to the negative consequences of ethnicity, while available data indicate that ethnicity may also be a source of strength. However, in either case, there is evidence of profound and consistent differences, in terms of a number of social and epidemiological indicators, among different ethnic groups.

For example, nonwhites experience higher mortality than white people at nearly every age. Consequently both nonwhite males and females have lower life expectancy at all ages, so proportionately fewer of them live to old age. At birth, white males can expect to live to 68.9 years of age, nonwhite males to age 62.9, white females to 76.6, and nonwhite females to 71.2 years of age. At age 60, life expectancy is 16.1 more years for white males and 15.4 for nonwhite males; for women, however, it is 20.8 more years for whites and 19.0 for nonwhites. It is important to note that there are smaller sex-specific differences in mortality among older nonwhites than whites. Consequently nonwhites have a more balanced sex ratio in old age than do whites: 79.9 men to every 100 women versus 71.6.[26] However, there is a secular trend toward greater differences in sex-specific mortality, at least among black people, so the differences may soon diminish and perhaps disappear.[27] There are also differences in cause-specific mortality. For example, among older people in the sixty-five to seventy-four-year-old age range, nonwhites are more than twice as likely to die of diabetes and cerebrovascular diseases than are their white counterparts.[28]

Other studies show ethnic differences in morbidity as well as mortality, especially morbidity associated with permanent disability and chronic disease. Table 5-1, which is based on national sample-survey data, shows that 40 percent of nonwhite respondents assessed their health as only fair or poor, compared with fewer than a third of whites. Local surveys among samples of older people in southern California and New York City, show substantially the same result: white people consistently rate their health more favorably than do nonwhites of the same age.[29] Moreover the southern California study included interviewers' assessments of respondents' health status. Once again white people's ratings were consistently higher than nonwhites'.[30] Table 5-1 indicates that both respondents and interviewers made realistic assessments because older nonwhite people appear more likely to be hypertensive and suffer major disabling conditions than white people and are likely to have experienced more than twice as many days of bed disability within the past year.

Table 5-1 also shows that nonwhite elderly receive less medical attention than their white counterparts although their need for medical care is at least

**Table 5-1**
**Selected Indicators by Race of Health of Older People**

| Self-Assessment of Health | White | All Minorities | Black Only |
|---|---|---|---|
| Health status self-report: fair or poor (percent) | 29 | 43 | 44 |
| Bed disability (days per year) | 11.7 | 24.6 | 24.6 |
| Persons with limitation of major activity (percent) | 40 | 50 | 51 |
| Prevalence of hypertension[a] (percent) | 39 | – | 55 |
| Physician visits (number per year) | 6.7 | 5.9 | 5.9 |

Source: U.S., Department of Health, Education and Welfare, *Health of the Disadvantaged: Chartbook* (Washington, D.C.: Public Health Service, 1977), pp. 63, 69, 73, 74, 79.

[a]Systolic: 160 mmHg; diastolic: 95 mmHg

as high. In spite or because of illness and disability minority aged make about 12 percent fewer visits to a physician annually than do whites. Moreover, as Cantor and Mayer found in their study of older people in New York City, to the extent that nonwhites seek medical attention, they are more likely to do so at hospital and outpatient departments, which tend to be their regular sources of care.[31]

There are also data that indicate ethnic differences in life style which, while not themselves mortality or morbidity indicators, have significant implication for older peoples' health. The Ten-State Nutrition Survey, which was undertaken between 1968 and 1970, compared the nutritional intake of black, white, and Spanish-speaking men and women, aged sixty or older.[32] While there were differences associated with gender and income, the study shows that white people generally have a higher nutritional intake than blacks and Spanish-Americans. Older blacks' diets are generally low in iron, calcium, and thiamine, while those of Spanish-speaking people lack vitamin A.[33] The survey also shows that older nonwhites particularly are more likely to have low or deficient values for hemoglobin, albumin, ascorbic acid, and vitamin C.[34] To a large extent this is a reflection of the lower income of the ethnic elderly. In 1975, according to Department of Health, Education and Welfare data, 36 percent of blacks and 33 percent of Spanish-speaking people sixty-five or older had incomes below the poverty level in comparison to 13.4 percent of the whites.

Minority older people are also at high risk of social and environmental stress. They generally have less education, live in lower-quality housing, and are less likely to own their homes than older whites. Moreover, the majority of older blacks and Hispanic elderly live in inner-city areas, where they are at high risk of such urban problems as crime and poor public services.[35]

Ethnicity is clearly associated with relatively high rates of late-life morbidity, mortality, and social stress. Of course ethnicity does not cause these
hardships but, as proponents of theories of multiple jeopardy have indicated,
the treatment that an ethnic group may receive from the majority society com-
pounds the risk.

There is evidence that ethnicity is not necessarily associated with disadvantage and disability. In economic terms there are relatively privileged ethnic
minorities, for example, Japanese-Americans.[36] Judged by certain standards,
older members of some relatively deprived minorities are in better physical or
emotional health than their more affluent white peers. Older black people are
more optimistic than white people, and there is some evidence that they have
higher morale. For example, in a comparative study of a sample of Anglo,
black, and Mexican-American residents in southern California, Bengtson et al.
found that black respondents, who were objectively at risk of higher mortality
than their white age-mates, were more likely to state that they believed that
they would live for ten years more.[37] Older blacks also have lower suicide
rates than older white persons, with particularly striking differences in sex-
specific rates. Older, black males are less than a third as likely to die by suicide
than white males of the same age.[38] There is a demographic crossover in race-
specific mortality; that is, very old cohorts of black people—those seventy-
five years old or older—have lower age-specific mortality rates than do their
white counterparts.[39]

There are a number of biological and psychological explanations for the
demographic crossover and the higher morale and lower suicide rates of older
blacks.[40] However, intriguing though they are, none adequately accounts for
the magnitude nor the direction of the differences which have been observed.
There has also been a series of sociological explanations: for example, the
members of minority groups show greater respect for older people than do
white people, the older members of these same minority groups participate
more fully in their communities, or they are more likely to receive support
from extended families or other kin.[41] Unfortunately these, too, are based
mainly on anecdotal or circumstantial evidence such as the fact that nonwhites
are underrepresented in long-term care facilities, and therefore hypothetically
are more frequently cared for by family or friends.[42]

To the extent that there are comparative data, they show there is no clear
relationship between ethnicity and community participation or social support.[43] For example, the National Council on Aging found that black people
fifty-five years old or older are slightly more likely to have attended a senior
citizens' center or Golden Age Club than their white counterparts (17 percent
versus 13 percent). What is more striking, of those who had not attended nearly
twice as many black respondents (39 percent versus 21 percent) expressed
interest in doing so.[44] On the other hand, Sterne and his colleagues found
that social-club membership among people in Rochester, New York, was related

to both sex and race. White males were more likely to join a social club than black males (27.5 percent versus 20.8 percent), but black females were most likely of all to join; more than twice as likely as white females (29.5 percent versus 14.5 percent).[45] In another study, Rubinstein has shown on the basis of national survey data that the social participation of older black people was not substantially different from that of whites.[46]

There is ample evidence that there are differences in the structure and function of ethnic families and that they have a significant impact on many aspects of domestic life.[47] However, there is no evidence that these differences are related to either the length or the quality of older peoples' lives.

As for the disadvantages observed among ethnic older people, there are several possible explanations. In some cases there is a direct intrinsic relationship, as when problems with language prevent people from receiving social service or health benefits to which they are entitled. In other cases, ethnicity influences behavior in more subtle ways, especially in the form of beliefs, attitudes, or values that either encourage harmful behavior or preclude seeking help in time of need. Nearly a quarter of Cheng's sample of Chinese-Americans reported that "lack of faith in doctors" was a major reason why older people do not seek medical care.[48] Valle and Mendoza report that a large proportion of their Latino sample in San Diego, California, hesitated or refused to go to physicians primarily not because they lacked money but because they feared bad news.[49] James Carter, a psychiatrist, contends that older black patients are reluctant to discuss fear, illness, and anxiety with white physicians because of an ethic that dictates that black people should appear content or at least stoic to white observers.[50]

Studies of other ethnic groups reach similar conclusions: that is, that group norms of self-reliance, stoicism, and mutual aid, which may not be forthcoming, interfere with the use of services by older adults. Carp, for example, investigated the low use of public housing for the elderly by Mexican-Americans in San Antonio, Texas. She found that, despite their apparent need for better housing, older Mexican-Americans did not want to live in an age-segregrated environment, although many of them felt that such housing was necessary and appropriate for other older adults.[51]

Alternatively the force of ethnicity on older peoples' behavior may be external. Health and social-service workers' prejudices or stereotypes of minority people, as well as older people, may inhibit their ability to provide adequate care or provide care in effective ways.[52]

As Bell et al. have noted, studies of multiple jeopardy must be interpreted with great caution to avoid confounding the effects of ethnicity with those of social class.[53] Indeed ethnicity in the United States, as in most settings, is closely related to class. With a few notable exceptions older nonwhite and non-English-speaking Americans are poorer, less educated, and more likely to have been employed in poorly-paid, low status occupations than their white counterparts.[54] These data reflect lifelong social and economic differences that have affected old age and the aging process in their own rights, independent of the effects of language, national origin, or race. Nevertheless their caveat notwithstanding, there appear to be more than chance associations between ethnicity and the health and social status of older adults.

### Old Age and Ethnicity: Policy Responses

Ethnic differences in the health and welfare of older people reflect lifelong differences in diet, occupation, education, and health care. For both immigrant and native-born minorities they also reflect the effects of years of persecution, privation, and personal hardship. While no programs or policies can eliminate these differences, they can alleviate some of their consequences and in that way improve the length and quality of late life. They can do so more effectively if they take account of the effect of ethnic differences on old age and aging, and if they are sufficiently flexible to alleviate the hardships and remove the barriers associated with ethnicity without, at the same time, compromising the strengths.

Policy makers and program administrators have begun to address the needs of minority aged, especially within the past ten years. However, in general, they have responded most consistently to only the more visible aspects of ethnicity, particularly those associated with deprivation and disability in old age.[55] For example, there are foreign-language guides to health and social services for those who cannot read English, and foreign-language radio and television public-service broadcasts for those who cannot read.[56] There are Title VII nutrition programs that accommodate both religious dietary restrictions and ethnic preferences for certain kinds of foods.[57] There have been efforts to build elderly housing projects that are consistent with indigenous architecture and with traditional ideas of landscape, style, and uses of space.[58] Medicare, Medicaid, and the Older Americans Act subsidize many ethnic organizations—church groups, women's groups, and philanthropic organizations that in turn provide a significant amount of long-term institutional and community-based care. There are no national data on the number of ethnic long-term care programs, but in the Greater Boston area these are presently nursing homes for older Norwegians, blacks, Germans, Armenians, Italians, Swedes, Greeks, and Jews, all of which are sponsored by nonprofit community groups and receive support from Medicare, Medicaid, or both.[59]

This is not to say that these efforts have eliminated the problems of minority aged nor even alleviated them to any significant degree. However, policymakers have at least identified significant problems and points of intervention, and in many cases they have demonstrated effective ways to intervene.

Policy initiatives have not recognized the more subtle relationships between ethnicity and aging, neither those associated with disability nor those
associated with strength, although there have been a few exemplary efforts.
The Determination of Need program in Massachusetts has recognized the importance of an ethnic ambiance—in terms of food, language, religion, and community participation—in approving applications for long-term care beds. The
Philadelphia Model Cities program made extensive use of indigenous community
workers in providing information and referral to older black, Puerto Rican,
foreignborn white elderly, apparently with considerable success.[60] A similar
effort, the *Servidor* program for Spanish-speaking older people in San Diego,
California, has endeavored to provide domiciliary care within the context
of traditional informal community support.[61]

These cases notwithstanding, there are still several policy needs and implications that have not yet been addressed. If black people, Spanish-speaking
people, and native Americans can expect to live, on the average, fewer than
sixty-five years, should they not be able to collect social security, Medicare,
and retirement benefits at younger ages? Or should they receive additional
care to enable them to live longer? At present they pay throughout their lifetimes for services that on the average they will never live to receive, although
their survivors will.[62]

If older Mexican-Americans do not want age-segregated housing nor any
public housing, then resources should be allocated to them for other kinds
of housing programs; for example, improvement or rehabilitation of the houses
in which they presently reside.

If, as Valle's and Mendoza's data indicate, fear inhibits older Mexican-
Americans from seeking medical attention, classical outreach programs and
information and referral are insufficient to increase their access to care. They
must be combined with special educational programs that carefully explain
the benefits of medical care and the risks of delay. There must also be special
educational programs for those who provide care to minority elderly, or, as
Carter has suggested, special efforts to train and recruit physicians, nurses,
social workers, and other health and welfare professionals who have the same
ethnic backgrounds as the older people themselves.

If older native Americans are disinclined to participate in congregate din-
ing or in other kinds of organized activities,[63] group-centered programs are
inappropriate for them. Home meals and individual visits or small group
activities may be more appropriate ways to meet their needs.

If Chinese or native American families are more reluctant than others
to place infirm parents or grandparents in nursing homes, then there should
be a greater concentration of resources on home-care alternatives. Correspondingly if community members, friends, and kin already care for frail, aged
neighbors or relatives, the goal of public policy should be the preservation

and augmentation of traditional supports rather than their replacement by public programs. Policy makers and administrators should beware lest bureaucratic programs inhibit or destroy informal community supports.

If older people associate with factions and schisms within their communities and if group members' interests are not monolithic, public policy should accommodate intragroup differences as well as those between ethnic groups. In practice this may engender considerable complication and inefficiency. There may be not one senior center, or social service agency, or nursing home for a particular ethnic community but two or more. However, it is most important that these differences be recognized in policy making. Older people may be less confortable in the company of people from rival factions than they would be with people of different ethnic backgrounds than their own. The essence of ethnicity is diversity, and public policy that tries to accommodate ethnic differences must respond to diverse needs, values, and goals.

There can be no global policy on ethnicity and aging. Programs for different ethnic groups must have different tactics and in many cases they will reflect different objectives. In some cases the objectives will be alien to those who formulate policy or implement programs.


**Conclusions**

For a number of reasons, it will be extraordinarily difficult (and expensive) to enact different programs for different ethnic groups. As Bell et al. have indicated, there are presently too few data to support strong conclusions about the conditions of minority older people much less suggest ways in which to accommodate public policy and service programs for their special needs.[64] There is a long agenda of new research on ethnicity and aging including:

1. Better vital statistics on ethnicity are needed. The present indicators of ethnicity, which are based on inconsistent and noncomparable criteria, are not adequate. For policy purposes, they must be replaced with more extensive data, including language, national origin, religion, and preferably some kind of self-identification.[65]
2. Epidemiological surveys of risks of mortality and morbidity associated with old age in different ethnic groups should be undertaken.
3. Needs assessments measuring the needs and the priorities of needs of older people of different ethnic backgrounds should be sufficiently refined, in terms of sampling, methods, and data analysis, to distinguish the influence of ethnicity from those of social class.
4. Studies of different cultures of aging, that is, intensive and extensive studies of differences in the social and psychological status of older people in different ethnic communities need to be done.[66]

5. Studies of older people in different ethnic milieux, that is, intensive and extensive studies of older people and the aging process in reference to changes in family roles, social supports, social responsibilities, and participation in community affairs would be useful.

This is not a new agenda.[67] What is more, it is an agenda which the National Institute on Aging and the Administration on Aging, to judge from their recent sets of research priorities, have already begun to address. There appears to be a commitment to policy based in part on ethnic differences—at least for the Spanish-speaking and nonwhites. Within a few years there will be the number and kind of data upon which sound policy decisions can be based.

However, data alone will not make or change policy. A social policy based on ethnic differences also poses tactical, ethical, and legal problems that no quantity of data can resolve. For example, policy makers and program administrators would have to recognize that people with different ethnic backgrounds have different perceptions and different priorities of needs. People may appear objectively to need one set of services or activities but may think that they need something else. Planners and administrators would have to show sufficient flexibility—and humility—to accommodate the needs of different communities, including those with which they may, in good faith, disagree.[68]

To many people it is morally repugnant to design programs or grant concessions to only selected groups of people even if these programs or concessions are clearly intended to redress the effects of historical wrongs. This has been true of Affirmative Action and Equal Opportunity programs, the main beneficiaries of which have been younger women and members of ethnic minorities, and it would certainly be true of programs for minority older adults. In the same way many people object to allocations of public funds to parochial organizations, including ethnic organizations, as violations of the separation of church and state. Special privilege, even as a response to extraordinary hardship, is offensive to many people and in some instances illegal, too.[69]

There are also political considerations. Ethnicity competes with other bases of social organizations and there is often conflict between the needs, or perceived needs, of different ethnic groups. Insofar as policy makers reinforce the strength of ethnic differences, they may inhibit the development of political organizations based on social class or the common problems of all older adults. From the perspective of political organizers, ethnic differences may be anachronistic barriers that public policy should try to eliminate rather than preserve.

There are serious practical problems with a social policy based on ethnicity. Who will define the ethnic groups in a given community and who will distinguish the critical factions within each group? What criteria will they use? How will policy makers accommodate the needs of small ethnic groups with small but needy older populations? How will policy accommodate those older people who choose not to associate themselves with an ethnic group?

There have been many discussions of aging and ethnicity, some of which show considerable sensitivity and insight, and many proposals for preserving the ethnic character of aging and old age. However, there have been few serious discussions of the legal, moral, and practical implications of a public policy that is committed to these ends. Ethnicity is more than pasta and soul food. For many older Americans, as for many younger ones, it is fundamental, a psychological, social, and historical fact of life that motivates their relationships with friends and family, government agencies, and other ethnic groups. A social policy based on ethnicity would in many ways be a sound and effective policy. However, such a policy would entail profound consequences, the implications of which have not been considered in adequate detail.

## Notes

1. There has been such an extensive literature on ethnicity within the past ten years that it is not possible to cite every relevant source. For thorough reviews, see, Ronald Cohen, "Ethnicity: Problem and Focus in Anthropology," *Annual Review of Anthropology* 7(1978):379-404; W.W. Isajiw, "Definitions of Ethnicity," *Ethnicity* 1(1974):111-124.

2. In reference to ethnicity in America, see, Richard Meister, ed., *Race and Ethnicity in Modern America* (Lexington, Mass.: Lexington Books, D.C. Heath and Co., 1974), and Andrew M. Greeley, *Ethnicity in the United States* (New York: Wiley, 1974).

There has been a number of conferences and symposia on the problems of minority older people in this country but, unfortunately, no comprehensive critical review. Rather, there has been a number of descriptive exploratory studies, most of which have been based on secondary sources or anecdotal accounts. The single most comprehensive study is Barbara Meyerhoff's *Number Our Days* (New York: Dutton, 1978).

Other useful studies include Margaret Clark and M. Mendelson, "Mexican-American Aged in San Francisco: a Case Description," *The Gerontologist* 9(1969):90-95; O.E. Leonard, "The Older Spanish-Speaking People of the Southwest," in *Older Rural Americans*, ed. E.G. Youmans (Lexington, Ky.: University of Kentucky Press, 1967), pp. 239-261; M. Powell Lawton, Morton H. Kleban, and Maurice Singer, "The Aged Jewish Person and the Slum Environment," *Journal of Gerontology* 26(1971):231-239; W.C. Swanson and C. L. Harter, "How Do Elderly Blacks Cope in New Orleans," *Aging and Human Development* 2(1971):210-216; J.J. Jackson, "The Blacklands of Gerontology," *Aging and Human Development* 2(1971):156-176.

In 1971 *The Gerontologist* published a number of papers dealing with minority aged (11:1, pt. 2); Joan W. Moore, "Mexican-Americans," pp. 30-35; Richard A. Kalish and Sam Yuen, "Americans of East Asian Ancestry: Aging and the Aged," pp. 36-47, and Donald P. Kent, "The Negro Aged," pp. 48-51.

There has recently been a *Cross-Cultural Study of Aging Minority Elders in San Diego*, the results of which have been published by The Campanile Press, under the general editorship of Ramon Valle. Individual volumes include: Frank Dukepoo, *The Elder American Indian*; E. Percil Stanford, *The Elder Black*; Eva Cheng, *The Elder Chinese*; Wesley H. Ishikawa, *The Elder Guamanian*; Karen C. Ishizuka, *The Elder Japanese*; Ramon Valle and Lydia Mendoza, *The Elder Latino;* Robert Paterson, *The Elder Filipino;* Wesley Ishikawa, *The Elder Samoan*. Each of these studies includes an extensive bibliography; for a separate bibliography on Spanish-speaking elderly, see, Maria Delgado and Gordon E. Finley, "The Spanish-Speaking Elderly: A Bibliography," *The Gerontologist* 18(1978):387-394.

Finally, there is a wealth of data, of highly uneven quality, in the proceedings of the 1971 White House Conference on Aging, and the U.S. Senate's Select Committee on Aging. The verbatim accounts have been published in a number of volumes by the Government Printing Office.

3. Unless otherwise indicated, "old" or "older", in this chapter, refers to people who are at least sixty-five years old.

4. For recent summaries of the demography of the older population, see, Neal E. Cutler and Robert A. Harootyan, "Demography of the Aged," in *Aging: Scientific Perspectives and Social Issues*, eds. Diana Woodruff and James E. Birren (New York: D. Van Nostrand Co., 1975), pp. 31-69. Jacob S. Siegel, "Demographic Aspects of Aging in the United States," in *Epidemiology of Aging*, eds. Adrian Ostfeld and Don C. Gibson (Washington, D.C.: Public Health Service, n.d.), pp. 17-82.

5. U.S., Department of Commerce, *Social and Economic Characteristics of the Older Population, 1974*, Current Population Reports, Special Studies Series P-23, no. 57 (Washington, D.C.: Bureau of the Census, 1975), p. 11.

6. Ibid, pp. 12-13.

7. Siegel, *Epidemiology of Aging*, pp. 34-51; Sam Stanley and Robert K. Thomas, "Current Demographic and Social Trends Among North American Indians," *Annals of the American Academy of Political and Social Sciences* 436 (1978):113; U.S., Department of Health, Education, and Welfare, "Social, Economic and Health Characteristics of Older American Indians," *Statistical Reports on Older Americans*, no. 4 (Washington, D.C.: Government Printing Office, 1978).

8. Laurence G. Branch, *Boston Elders: A Survey of Needs* (Boston: Commission on Affairs of the Elderly/Area Agency on Aging, Region VI, 1978), pp. 140-141.

9. U.S., Department of Health, Education, and Welfare, "Some Prospects for the Future Elderly Population," *Statistical Reports on Older Americans, no. 3* (Washington, D.C.: Administration on Aging, 1978), p. 11.

10. For example, Valle and Mendoza, *The Elder Latino*, pp. 43-44; Ishizuka, *The Elder Samoan*, p. 11; Cheng, *The Elder Chinese*, p. 14.

11. John D. Cormican, "Breaking the Language Barrier Between the Patient and His Doctor," *Geriatrics* 23(1975):104-110.

12. U.S., Commission on Civil Rights, *Counting the Forgotten: the 1970 Census Count of Persons of Spanish-Speaking Background in the United States* (Washington, D.C.: Government Printing Office, 1974), pp. 2, 34-40, 44-47.

13. Ibid., pp. 44-45.

14. Ibid., pp. 56-86. Although government documents continue to use these criteria of ethnicity, there is a grudging recognition of their inadequacy. For example, the "Race/Ethnicity" section of the Long-Term Health Care Minimum Data Set, which uses the census categories, includes the following note: "The above categories were chosen because they are the ones promulgated by the Office of Management and Budget for government-wide use. The panel recognizes that it may be desirable in some parts of the country to expand this minimum classification." U.S., Department of Health, Education, and Welfare, National Center for Health Statistics, *Long-Term Health Care Minimum Data Set*, (Washington, D.C.: Public Health Service, 1979), p. 13.

15. Jacqueline Jackson has made this point most emphatically in reference to Black Americans; "Aged Negroes: Their Cultural Departures from Statistical Stereotypes," *The Gerontologist* 10(1970):140-145; "Sex and Social Class Variations in Black and Parent-Child Relationships," *Aging and Human Development* 2(1971):96-107; "Negro Aged, Toward Needed Research in Social Gerontology," *The Gerontologist* 11(1971):52-57.

16. Cheng, *The Elder Chinese*, pp. 16, 27; Valle and Mendoza, *The Elder Latino*, p. 48; Stanford, *The Elder Black*, p. 17.

17. Ishizuka, *The Elder Japanese*, pp. 17, 20-21, 25-26; Stanford, *The Elder Black*, pp. 23-24.

18. Lawton, Kleban, and Singer, "Aged Jewish Person"; Stanford, *The Elder Black*, p. 27. In this same regard, Branch's data indicates significant concentration of older Orientals, Blacks, Jews, Italians, and Irish in various Boston neighborhoods (Branch, *Boston Elders*, pp. 140-141).

19. Ishizuka, *The Elder Japanese*, pp. 25-26.

20. Ibid., pp. 35-39.

21. Meyerhoff, *Number Our Days*, pp. 7-11.

22. Ibid., pp. 153-194.

23. Ibid., pp. 232-268.

24. National Urban League, *Double Jeopardy: The Older Negro in America Today* (Washington, D.C.: National Urban League, 1964).

25. For example, see, National Council on Aging, *Triple Jeopardy: Myth or Reality* (Washington, D.C.: National Council on Aging, 1972); Sharon Fujii,

"Older Asian Americans: Victims of Multiple Jeopardy," *Civil Rights Digest* 9(1976):25-34.

26. Cutler and Harootyan, *Aging*, pp. 50-51.

27. Siegel, *Epidemiology of Aging*, pp. 51-54.

28. However, these and other differences seem to disappear and even reverse at older ages. Siegel, *Epidemiology of Aging*, pp. 56-57.

29. The California study is reported in V.L. Bengtson, P.L. Kasschau, and P.K. Ragan, "Environmental and Health Influences on Aging and Behavior," in *Handbook of the Psychology of Aging*, eds. James E. Birren and K. Werner Schaie (New York: Van Nostrand, 1977), p. 340. The New York data appear in Marjorie Cantor and Mary Mayer, "Health and the Inner-City Elderly," *The Gerontologist* 16(1976):19.

30. Bengtson, Kasschau, and Ragan, *Psychology of Aging*, p. 340.

31. Cantor and Mayer, "Health and the Inner-City Elderly", pp. 20-22.

32. Robert E. Shank, "Nutrition and Aging," in *Epidemiology of Aging*, eds. Adrian Ostfeld and Don C. Gibson, (Washington, D.C.: Public Health Service, n.d.), pp. 199-213.

33. Ibid., pp. 205-208.

34. Ibid., pp. 207-210.

35. Cantor and Mayer, "Health and the Inner-City Elderly"; Siegel, *Epidemiology of Aging*, pp. 48-51; M. Margaret Clark, "Patterns of Aging Among the Elderly Poor of the Inner City," *The Gerontologist* 11(1971): 58-66; Richard S. Sterne, James Phillips and A. Rabuska, *The Urban Elderly Poor* (Lexington, Mass.: D.C. Heath Co., 1974), pp. 11-28.

36. Jerry Weaver, "Personal Health Care: a Major Concern for Minority Aged," in *Comprehensive Service Delivery Systems for the Minority Aged*, Proceedings of the Fourth Institute on Minority Aging (San Diego, Calif.: Center on Aging, 1977), pp. 46-47.

37. Bengtson, Kasschau, and Ragan, *Psychology of Aging*, pp. 340-341.

38. Davor Jedlicka, Yongsock Shin, and Everett S. Lee, "Suicide among Blacks," *Phylon* 38(1977):448-454.

39. Kenneth Manton, Sharon Sandomirsky Poss and Steven Wing, "Black/ White Mortality Crossover: Investigation from the Perspectives of the Components of Aging," *The Gerontologist* 19(1979):291-300.

40. David K. Reynolds and Richard A. Kalish, "Anticipation of Futurity as a Function of Ethnicity and Age," *Journal of Gerontology* 27(1974):224-231; Manton, Poss and Wing, "Black/White Mortality Crossover" pp. 291-294.

41. These statements appear frequently in the proceedings of conferences on minority aging, of which there have been a number in the past decade. Though usually undocumented or poorly documented, they have had a significant influence on academic gerontology. For example, Robert Butler, *Why Survive? Being Old in America* (New York: Harper, 1975), pp. 31-32; Robert Butler and Myrna Lewis, *Aging and Mental Health*, 2nd ed. (St. Louis: Mosby, 1977), p. 94.

For a thoughtful critical review, see, Carol E. Woehrer, "Cultural Pluralism in American Families: The Impact of Ethnicity on Social Aspects of Aging," *The Family Coordinator* 27(1978):329-339.

42. U.S., Department of Health, Education, and Welfare, "Characteristics, Social Contacts and Activities of Nursing Home Residents," *Vital and Health Statistics,* Series 13, no. 27 (Washington, D.C.: Public Health Service, 1977), pp. 3-4.

43. For a summary evaluation of these assertions, see Bengtson, Kasschau, and Ragan, *Psychology of Aging*, pp. 342-343.

44. Louis Harris Associates, *The Myth and Reality of Aging in America* (Washington, D.C.: National Council on Aging, 1975), pp. 184-187.

45. Sterne, *Urban Elderly Poor*, pp. 30-31.

46. Daniel I. Rubinstein, "An Examination of Social Participation among a National Sample of Black and White Elderly," *Aging and Human Development* 2(1971):172-189. Ehrlich also reports lower life satisfaction and social participation in his study of "Black and White Elderly in St. Louis." However, his sample was limited to those who were at least seventy years old, in "fair, good, or excellent" health, and with incomes in excess of $1,200 per year. Ira Ehrlich, "Toward a Social Profile of the Aged Black Population in the United States: An Exploratory Study," *International Journal of Aging and Human Development* 4(1973):271-276.

47. For example in reference to urban black families, see, Carol B. Stack, *All Our Kin* (New York: Harper, 1975), pp. 32-107.

48. Cheng, *The Elder Chinese*, p. 15.

49. Valle and Mendoza, *The Elder Latino*, p. 51.

50. James Carter, "Recognizing Psychiatric Symptoms in Black Americans," *Geriatrics* 22(1974):95-99.

51. Frances M. Carp, "Housing and Minority–Group Elderly" *The Gerontologist* 9(1969):22-23.

52. Butler and Lewis, *Aging and Mental Health*, pp. 92-99.

53. Barbara Solomon, "Better Planning thru Research" in *Comprehensive Service Delivery Systems for the Minority Aged*, ed. E. Percil Stanford (San Diego, Calif.: Campanile Press, 1977), pp. 22-23, 26-28.

54. National Urban League, *Double Jeopardy.*

55. The most comprehensive summary of service programs for minority aged is a RAND Corporation report: Durran Bell, Patricia Kasschau, and Gail Zellman, *Delivery Services to Elderly Members of Minority Groups: a Critical Review of the Literature* (Santa Monica, Calif.: The RAND Corporation, 1976), cited by Solomon, "Better Planning through Research," pp. 19-30.

The most comprehensive agenda appears in the summary statements of the 1971 White House Conference on Aging. Of the *Recommendations for Action*, four deal with the problems of nonwhite older adults: *The Aging and Aged Blacks, The Elderly Indian, The Spanish-Speaking Elderly,* and *The Asian-American Elderly.* All of these reports were published by the Government Printing Office in 1972.

56. U.S., Congress, Senate, Special Committee on Aging, *Availability and Usefulness of Federal Programs and Services to Older Mexican-Americans,* (Washington, D.C.: Government Printing Office, 1969), p. 311.

57. For example, Janet Levy, "Minority Aging—Services Respond to their Cultural Needs," in *Comprehensive Service Delivery Systems for the Minority Aged,* ed. E. Percil Stanford (San Diego, Calif.: Campanile Press, 1977), pp. 8-9

58. Carp, "Housing and Minority—Group Elderly" p. 20.

59. Women's Industrial and Educational Union, *Levels of Care Facilities in Massachusetts, 1977,* (Boston, Mass.: Women's Industrial and Educational Union, 1977).

60. Donald P. Kent and Carl Hirsch, "Indigenous Workers as a Crucial Link in the Total Support System for Low-Income, Minority Group Aged: A Report of an Innovative Field Technique in Survey Research," *Aging and Human Development* 2(1971):189-196.

61. Valle and Mendoza, *The Elder Latino,* pp. 70-73.

62. Michael Gilfix, "Minority Elders: Legal Problems and the Need for Legal Services," in *Comprehensive Service Delivery Systems for the Minority Aged,* ed. E. Percil Stanford (San Diego, Calif.: Campanile Press, 1977), pp. 134-136.

63. Gaea Duncan, "The Inter-Tribal Council of California, Inc.," in *Comprehensive Service Delivery Systems for the Minority Aged,* ed. E. Percil Stanford (San Diego, Calif.: Campanile Press, 1977), p. 149.

64. Solomon, *Comprehensive Service Delivery Systems.*

65 U.S., Commission on Civil Rights, *Counting the Forgotten,* pp. 7-8. If fixed response categories are used, they must be carefully pretested to be as exhaustive as they can. Even Branch, who allowed six choices of ethnicity, found that 30 percent of his sample described themselves as members of an "other" ethnic group (Branch, *Boston Elders,* p. 140).

66. Compare, M. Margaret Clark and Barbara G. Anderson, *Culture and Aging: an Anthropological Study of Older Americans* (Springfield, Ill.: Charles Thomas, 1967).

67. Solomon, *Comprehensive Service Delivery Systems;* Kent, "Indigenous Workers"; Jackson, "Negro Aged"; Christie W. Kiefer, "Notes on Anthropology and the Minority Elderly," *The Gerontologist* 11(1971):94-98.

68. Compare, Solomon, *Comprehensive Service Delivery Systems,* pp. 21-24.

69. Ibid.

# Education and Public Policy for Older Adults

*Stanley M. Grabowski*

The anomaly is that a nation with a rapidly increasing cohort of older people is doing so little for the education of older adults. Older adults are the fastest growing minority in the nation, both in whole numbers and percentages. Currently there are about 25 million people sixty-five and over in the United States. Although they comprise only about 11 percent of the population, numerically they are more than the entire population of Canada. Demographic predictions point to a steady rise in the numbers and percentages of older adults into the middle of the next century.

These staggering statistics become more meaningful and crucial to the needs of older adults when examined against the educational background and current participation patterns of older adults in educational offerings of all types. Only 8 percent of older adults have completed high school, and the rest have had less than a high school education, with perhaps as many as 10 percent totally illiterate.[1]

It is not surprising that older adults do not participate in educational programs. Currently less than one-half million or 2.4 percent of all adults sixty-five years old and over participate in adult education programs.[2] This figure is predictably very low when compared with the participation of the general adult population. Various studies have clearly shown that there is a positive correlation between the level of one's education and participation in education programs.[3]

Aside from a lack of formal schooling, there are other reasons why older adults do not participate in educational programs. One reason affecting even those who have had more exposure to schooling is the lack of motivation to participate in any formal learning endeavors. Often older adults have an attitude of, "Why do I need any more education? What can it do for me? After all, I have survived up to this point on what I have by way of education; why do I need more?" For such adults education is a pointless option because they do not see it as relevant to their needs or interests. They "regard education as something separate and different from the programs of other service areas with which they are more familiar."[4]

Another reason why older adults do not participate in educational programs is that they have subscribed to the myth that they are too old to learn.

Some older adults have unpleasant memories of their childhood education that prevent them from participating during their later years.

In addition there are real barriers to their participation in the form of costs, transportation, services, scheduling, and information. By the kinds of obstructions put in the way of older adults and not programming for their needs and interests, educational institutions generally do not encourage older adults to participate. In the past, institutions of higher education have not taken older adults seriously as bona fide clients.[5] Accurate, up-to-date statistics on how many colleges and universities are offering special programs for older adults are not available, but the number may be under 1,000, representing less than a third of all the institutions of higher learning in the nation.[6]

It may be that institutions of higher education are not clear what purpose education has for older adults and how that purpose would fit into the overall context of youth education. Also the fear that programs for older adults might siphon dwindling resources bolsters an out-and-out prejudice against older people.

One study found that the main obstacles educational providers listed as inhibiting expansion of programs for older adults were (in rank order): (1) finance, 57 percent; (2) inadequate supportive services, 40 percent; (3) shortage of trained staff, 38 percent; (4) lack of interest on the part of older people, 32 percent; (5) locating or contacting an appropriate audience, 26 percent; and (6) cost to participants, 17 percent.[7]

This shameful condition makes it all the more imperative to establish and follow a more positive policy with regard to the educational opportunities for older adults. Older adults are not only disadvantaged by biological and physiological decrements, but they are also stigmatized and isolated from the rest of society by myths, stereotypes, and age-segregated policies. Even those who are supposed to care, provide for, and protect older adults—those who are included in the so-called aging network, such as physicians, personnel in hospitals and long-term-care institutions, social security administrators, and other governmental bureaucrats—are often more involved in fighting for the largest share of available resources rather than the welfare of their clients.[8]

The paradox that older adults need more not less education seems to be lost on most of us but especially on legislators and policy makers. Lack of education for older adults is far more serious for them than the general public realizes. "Today there is a cruel and ironic contradiction in the fate of our older citizens. Never before have older people been able to look forward to so many years of vitality. But never before have they been so firmly shouldered out of every significant role in life—in the family, in the world of work, and in the community."[9]

Sheer survival is the harvest older adults will reap for lack of continuing learning in an era when they, and their skills, are culturally obsolete. Not having the habit of learning may be connected with self-deprecating and self-depriving tendencies that constrict life and make it less tolerable and enduring.[10] This is dramatized repeatedly where ignorance of current knowledge may lead to misery, infirmity, and even to death through failure to cope with problems, difficulties, and conditions regarding personal health and safety, and the quality of life. Education for older adults is necessary if one is to be kept informed and able to relate to society's rapid changes.

In addition most older adults are not ready to disengage totally from the mainstream of life and activities. They want to remain alert and active by being productive and useful. Many want to continue using their skills as well as acquire new ones. If nothing else, they are interested in learning how to cope with the transition to retirement. A small number even want to pursue college degrees which they did not have a chance to earn during their earlier years. In any case, the later years of life present an opportunity for integration or summing up, for seeking the meanings that have been avoided or postponed, which education can facilitate.[11]

Education for older adults gained a greater legitimacy following the 1971 White House Conference on Aging but not by much. Institutions of higher education are becoming more receptive to older adults. However, this greater receptivity is not only in recognition that continued education is necessary throughout life but also represents a search for a new clientele to make up for dwindling enrollments of traditional eighteen- to twenty-two-year-old students.[12]

Of all educational institutions, community colleges, particularly those supported with public funds, have taken the leadership in providing educational opportunities for older adults. In accordance with their philosophies and community perspective, they may be the best ones to serve the educational needs of the majority of older adults.

Aside from educational institutions many other agencies, organizations, and institutions are making efforts to provide educational programs for older adults. One recent survey indicated that 3,500 agencies have some kind of program in the area of education for older adults. These agencies include voluntary associations, community agencies, churches, synagogues, YMCAs and YWCAs, senior-citizen centers, Cooperative Extension Service, libraries, museums, public schools, business, industry, labor unions, park and recreation departments, and older adult membership associations. By and large these offerings are uncoordinated; many are transient and represent specific interests and capacities of the organizations offering them rather than careful needs assessments of the potential students.

But in spite of barriers to participation in education programs, incomplete planning, and the dearth of such offerings in some locales, older adults are engaged in learning on their own. Most adults, including older adults, conduct some sort of systematic inquiry through self-directed learning projects. About three-fourths of these are totally planned by the learner and less than 1 percent of such undertakings are motivated by academic credit.[13] Furthermore, almost 85 percent of older adults engage in such projects, spending on an average nearly 325 hours a year in these pursuits.[14]

## What Needs to be Done

The present state of affairs is not adequate. It needs to be changed dramatically. What is it that needs to be done? To answer that question it is necessary to consider the function and role of education in our society and how it applies to older adults.

Learning has been called an "adjustment instrument" for all age groups in society. One of the major functions of education is to provide everyone with the capacity to participate actively in a society that is in constant flux and change. Education thus helps individuals to grow personally and socially.[15] If this is the case, then older adults—as does everyone in our society—have a right to education, as was noted by the Council of Chief State School Officers: "A free public education is everyone's right. It shall not be denied to any person regardless of age.... A wide range of life-long educational opportunities must be made available to all citizens of this nation so that the fundamental rights and responsibilities of free choice may be learned and exercised with regard to each individual's future."[16]

This right to education was also expressed in the final report of the 1971 White House Conference on Aging. "Education is a basic right for all persons of all age groups. It is continuous and henceforth one of the ways enabling older people to have a full and meaningful life, and is a means of helping them develop their potential as a resource for the betterment of society."[17] The same expression appeared in a "bill of rights" for the life-long learner drawn up by the assembly of the American Association of Community and Junior Colleges:

> Every adult American has the right to continue to learn throughout life;
>
> Every adult American has the right to equal opportunity for access to relevant learning opportunities at each stage of life;
>
> Diversity and access to educational opportunity are important to democracy in the United States;
>
> Any index of the quality of life in the United States includes opportunities for growth and self-actualization as a right of the learning society;
>
> Neither age, nor sex, nor color, nor creed, nor ethnic background, nor marital status, nor economic status, nor disability should create barriers to the opportunity to continue to grow through participation in organized learning activities;
>
> Coping, living, and working are dimensions which exemplify the range of learning needs of the learning society;
>
> Public investment in the learning society is an investment in human capital and in human condition.[18]

If we subscribe to these declarations about the right of all individuals to education, why is it that some people call it a myth?[19] The answer may lie in economics; the usefulness of education is measured by its impact on the gross national product, and, since most older adults are unemployed, there may appear to be little reason to spend money on their education. The only slight concession is made where educational programs for older adults are vocational or occupational.[20]

Even if one were to accept such reasoning, one could argue a strong case to support more education for older adults. The recent development of *social indicators*, broad measurements of productive living as a barometer of the welfare of the country, point to a day in the very near future when older adults will be urged to return to the workforce.[21] Peter Drucker, addressing the Thirty-first Conference of the American Society of Training and Development, predicted that in the early 1980s there would be a shortage of workers. The talents, experiences, and resourcefulness of our older adults are a national asset not yet used to advantage. If we are to tap them for a return to the labor force, we will have to provide them with some educational programs to update their skills in line with today's technology and its demands.

However, apart from educational opportunities to retool themselves for the labor market, older adults ought to have a right to pursue education strictly for leisure purposes. Many older adults find that leisure has a meaning only in relation to work and other activities. Leisure without some meaningful activity often results in depression and listlessness. Today's older adults can look forward to fifteen or twenty years of healthy retirement—much too long a period to spend in perpetual leisure.[22]

The value of education for older adults has been categorized by McClusky to encompass the following:

Coping needs are basic education and education for health and economic self-sufficiency, which are required to function in society;

Expressive needs is the need to enrich one's living, including activities that are for the sake of the activity itself, for the sheer pleasure itself;

Contributive needs is the desire to be of service; to contribute something acceptable to others and to the community;

Influence needs refers to exerting an influence on one's own circumstances of living and one's environment; and

Transcendence needs means to rise above one's condition and continue one's self-development.[23]

Older adults can use education not only to meet their immediate needs and interests and those of society but to find new roles and options for the later years.[24] Education—which literally means to lead or draw out—need not focus only on helping older adults adjust to the commonly accepted limitations of age and accept normatively expected patterns of living and behavior. It may also serve as an agent of becoming and transcending the culturally accepted and expected.[25]

It is obvious that the United States can no longer deal with the older population and with succeeding older adults in the ways it has in the past. Traditional ways and conventional policies must give way to new directions, policies, and priorities that will enable older adults to use their talents best, satisfy their needs and interests, and be contributing members of society. The new approaches must be multidimensional and all-embracing, but they must give a high priority to education of older adults as well as education of all sectors of our society. The quality of response to these problems and challenges will depend in large measure on the competencies of those working with older adults, an implication that the training and education of the service providers is also a consideration under any policies regarding education of older adults.

If older adults have a right to education, if they need education to cope in a rapidly changing society that is also a learning society, and if the economic well-being of this nation will depend on more older adults reentering or remaining in the labor force, a more specific policy regarding education for older adults must be established. Whatever policy is devised—and that will be an evolutionary process—it must address short-range and long-range goals for those who have already reached their later years and those who will do so in the future. In addition, such a policy ought to encompass education about aging for persons of all ages. As the United Nations report on the trends and policies toward the aging noted in 1975:

> It is important that specific goals be articulated as a basis for long-range and short-range planning and resource and programme development. Broad policy goals in regard to the elderly should be stated in such a way as to recognize their special rights in society and to identify specific and general responsibilities of government towards older persons . . . , such goals must be defined within a framework of the implications of aging and of being aged for the individual, the family, the community and the society . . . based upon an understanding of the nature of aging. It should also include aging as an intergenerational concept, i.e., that the understanding of growing old and the condition of being old are related to a specific generation within its historical, cultural, and developmental context.[26]

Such a framework would enable development of a fundamental understanding of the life span, without which a public policy toward education for and about the aged would be time and culture bound. Parenthetically, one must note that "in the narrow frame of reference within which Washingtonians revel, the word 'policy' has a here and now cast to it which virtually prohibits looking at anything further ahead than eighteen months."[27] To the extent possible, public policy must eschew the here and now expediency in education for and about older adults.

McClusky has summarized the long-range goals of education for older people as growth in fulfillment of lifetime potential; development of abilities uniquely available in the later years; facilitating the service of the old as models for emulation and guidance of oncoming generations; acceptance by all of the desirability, legitimacy, and feasibility of these goals; promoting continuing opportunity in lifelong learning; provision of specialized programs to meet the particular needs of the old; and delivery of educational programs to those who are nonparticipants and isolated from the mainstream of community services.[28]

If one judges by the existing legislation in this area, this country still has a negative policy toward older adults in the realm of education. Technically it is true that older adults are covered by legislation that deals with all adults across the board, but in practice older adults have been treated as less than second-rate citizens under these laws. Even the Older Americans Act of 1965 did not specifically mention education until the 1973 revisions. Education for older adults has been neglected by what has been called "the politics of non-consideration." As Stanford and Dolar commented, "It is precisely because education for older adults is not vocationally or economically rewarding that federal legislation has been negligible in this regard."[29]

Hopefully future cohorts of older adults will age differently from the way it happened in the past and the way current older adults are aging vis-à-vis society. They (we) will be more actively involved, less willing to sit back and watch passively. The impact of advisory groups, such as the Gray Panthers, will be more active and influential in politics and community affairs.[30]

Older Americans will shape the platforms and views of candidates running for elected office, especially for Congress and the Senate, toward more responsive educational policies. Through the generation of debates and discussions the policy apparatus will be forced to take their views and needs into account.[31]

Policy development is a complex process. No one group can ordinarily bring it about without cooperation of others. Indeed policy development is often more a concatenation of "squeaky wheels, personality, and sheer political opportunism (certainly not always partisan, either), although on the margins it is possible for the application of logic and reason to have some effect."[32]

Laws are not sufficient by themselves to insure fair and adequate educational opportunities for older adults. Realistically laws may not be implemented for a long time, if ever, for lack of appropriations. Also, laws may remain inert for lack of public interest in them. Much depends on how well the educational needs of older adults are perceived and appreciated by diverse sectors of society, such as legislators, academicians, social and service agencies, and older adults themselves.

The White House Conference on Aging made numerous recommendations regarding education, most of which have not yet been fully implemented. Among the major recommendations were the following:

Older adults should be involved in planning programs destined for them;

More educational opportunities should be provided for older adults to fit their needs, interests, and special circumstances;

Providers of education ought to offer incentives for older adults, especially by eliminating barriers to their participation;

Create a national awareness and better understanding by society of the needs of older adults;

Higher priorities should be established for education of older adults, especially in the form of increased money and human resources in accordance with the proportion of older adults in the general population.[33]

The long-range goals of "education should be regarded as a program to which all other aspects of living in the later years should be related."[34] However, long-range goals, important as they may be, must be supplemented and augmented by short-range goals that touch on the lives of the current cohort of older adults.

Among the pressing short-range goals must be the provision of remedial and basic education to the hundreds of thousands of older adults who have had little or no education. Most older adults who have had no more than an elementary education probably received it prior to 1920 when teachers and institutional facilities were less than adequate. Much of what was taught then is obsolescent in today's world.[35]

Yet providing this kind of education can touch very sensitive areas in older adults. Remedial education is never on the top of any list of learning priorities among older adults. It is generally closer to the bottom of such lists. Nevertheless it should be available as an option to older adults even if they choose not to exercise it. Perhaps there is a far greater urgency to apply educational remedies to forestall repetitions of such conditions among future age cohorts. In a polemic on this issue, Ecklund stated that "Although some remedial and basic education may still be possible with a portion of this group, their situation of relative disadvantage should generate a resolve to prevent such disadvantage among succeeding generations."[36]

Another short-range goal has to do with an extension of educational opportunities to older adults. Many steps can be taken immediately in this regard. More of the existing programs can be opened to older adults. Some public and private institutions are allowing and even encouraging older adults to participate in their regular offerings. Some allow them to take courses for credit at no cost or reduced tuition rates; others allow them to participate only on a "space available" basis; others restrict them to auditing or taking courses that are not for credit.

Another way institutions can make it easier for older adults to participate in educational programs is to inform them of what is offered  and provide support services such as counseling, transportation, outreach programs, and a variety of learning approaches. These supportive services will have to be supported economically through public and private sources. In addition, institutions can offer programs designed especially for needs indigenous to older adults.

Another short-range goal, which will have a long-range payoff, is in the area of research. There is a need to develop instructional materials for older adults and for staff training, as well as for ways to locate resources and assistance for education of older adults. Ansello and Hayslip summarized the tasks ahead:

> Higher-education researchers can investigate ways of: (1) improving instructional techniques to bring learning closer to home; (2) exploring new careers for older workers; (3) retraining older teachers to meet new community educational needs; (4) using retired professors in the design and conduct of older-adult education programs; and (5) creating older-adult peer teacher corps in higher education to provide counsel and to design meaningful curricula for older adults.[37]

A final short-range goal impinging on the future is the infusion of information about aging as a normal process into school curricula at all levels. Education must be seen and felt as a truly lifelong process. It is not enough to mouth the platitudes that are usually heard about career education and lifelong learning. We must translate that philosophy into practice so that today's youth will be prepared to continue their learning throughout life and will demand that government at all levels make it possible for present and future older adults to do so.

## Notes

1. Ruth Weinstock, *The Graying of the Campus* (New York: Educational Facilities Laboratories, 1978).

2. Academy for Educational Development, *Never Too Old To Learn* (New York: Academy for Educational Development, 1974).

3. John W.C. Johnstone and Ramon J. Rivera, *Volunteers for Learning* (Chicago: Aldine Publishing Co., 1965).

4. *Toward a National Policy on Aging*, Proceedings of the 1971 White House Conference on Aging, November 28-December 2, Washington, D.C., vol. II, Conference Findings and Resolutions from the Sections and Special Concerns Sessions (Washington, D.C.: Government Printing Office, 1973), p. 3.

5. Weinstock, *The Graying of the Campus.*

6. John Scanlon, *How to Plan a College Program for Older People.* (New York: Academy for Educational Development, 1978).

7. Roger DeCrow, *New Learning for Older Americans: An Overview of National Effort* (Washington, D.C.: Adult Education Association of the U.S.A., n.d.), p. 70.

8. Carroll L. Estes, *The Aging Enterprise* (San Francisco: Jossey-Bass, 1979).

9. John Gardner, *No Easy Victories* (New York: Harper and Row, 1968), p. 153.

10. Edward E. Marcus, "The Educational Plight of Today's Elderly", 1972.

11. Ronald H. Sherron and D. Barry Lumsden, eds., *Introduction to Educational Gerontology* (Washington, D.C.: Hemisphere Publishing, 1978).

12. Ibid.

13. Allen Tough, *The Adult Learning Projects: A Fresh Approach to Theory and Practice in Adult Learning* (Toronto, Ontario: Institute for Studies in Education, 1971).

14. Roger P. Hiemstra, *The Older Adult and Learning* (Lincoln: University of Nebraska, 1975).

15. Lillian L. Glickman, Benjamin S. Hersey, and Ira I. Goldenberg, *Community Colleges Respond to Elders* (Washington, D.C.: Department of Health, Education, and Welfare, 1975).

16. Council of Chief State School Officers, *Policy Statements* (Washington, D.C., Council of Chief State School Officers, 1976).

17. *Toward A National Policy on Aging*, p. 6.

18. Jamison Gilder, ed., *Policies for Lifelong Learning. Report of the 1979 Assembly American Association of Community and Junior Colleges* (Washington, D.C.: American Association of Community and Junior Colleges, 1979), p. 113.

19. Sherron and Lumsden, *Introduction to Educational Gerontology.*

20. Ibid.

21. DeCrow, *New Learning for Older Americans.*

22. Glickman, Hersey, and Goldenberg, *Community Colleges Respond*, p. 3.

23. Howard Y. McClusky, "Education for Aging: The Scope of the Field and Perspectives for The Future," in *Learning for Aging*, eds. Stanley M. Grabowski and W. Dean Mason (Washington, D.C.: Adult Education Association of the U.S.A., 1974).

24. Glickman, Hersey, and Goldenberg, *Community Colleges Respond*, p. 3.

25. Ibid.

26. United Nations, Department of Economic and Social Affairs, *The Aging: Trends and Policies* (New York: United Nations, 1975), p. 53.

27. Hendrik D. Gideonse, "Can the Federal Government Use the Futures Perspective?" *Notes on the Future of Education* 3(1972):5.

28. Howard Y. McClusky and the Technical Committee on Education, *Education, Background and Issues*, 1971 White House Conference on Aging (Washington, D.C.: Government Printing Office, 1971).

29. E. Percil Stanford and Antonia Dolar, "Federal Policy in Education for Older Adults," in *Introduction to Educational Gerontology*, eds. Ronald H. Sherron and D. Barry Lumsden (Washington, D.C.: Hemisphere Publishing, 1978), pp. 131-153.

30. Glickman, Hersey, and Goldenberg, *Community Colleges Respond.*

31. Gideonse, "Futures Perspective," p. 5.

32. Ibid., p. 6.

33. Summarized from *Toward A National Policy on Aging*, p. 3.

34. Ibid.

35. McClusky, *Education, Background and Issues.*

36. Lowell Ecklund, "Aging and the Field of Education," in *Aging and Society, vol. 2, Aging and the Professions*, eds. Matilda Riley, John W. Riley, Jr., and Marilyn Johnson (New York: Russell Sage Foundation, 1969), pp. 3-9.

37. Edward F. Ansello and Bert Hayslip, Jr., "Older Adult Higher Education: Stepchild and Cinderella." in *Gerontology in Higher Education: Developing Institutional and Community Strength*, eds. Harvey L. Sterns, Edward F. Ansello, Betsy M. Sprouse, and Ruth Layfield-Faux (Belmont, Calif.: Wadsworth, 1979), p. 270.

# 7

## Portrait of a Phenomenon—the Gray Panthers: Do They Have a Long-Run Future?

*Ruth H. Jacobs*

The 1977 Gray Panthers' National Convention was of interest to me both as a sociologist and as a midlife woman. The Gray Panthers present a series of paradoxes. They are radical, yet composed of predominantly old people whom researchers have traditionally described as conservative.[1] They use tactics of the 1960s yet have survived through 1979. Their leader is a charismatic woman who urges individual membership autonomy. They are a national organization yet have only recently begun to have any semblance of a formal organizational structure. In the following pages, drawing from my observation, media coverage about their activities, and their own words, the membership and work of the Panthers and of Maggie Kuhn are highlighted to shed light on the question: Do the Gray Panthers have a long-range future as agents for social change?

### Who are the Gray Panthers?

It is only nine years since Maggie Kuhn and six Philadelphia friends, angered at their mandatory retirement from religious and social-service organizations, aligned themselves with disenchanted young people to create the Gray Panthers. Yet a cabbie driving speaker Studs Terkel from the Washington, D.C., airport to their 1977 national convention recognized the name Gray Panthers and asked "Aren't they violent?" "I answered, 'You bet they are,'" Studs told the conventioneers. The 400 Panthers laughed with delight at the recognition of their refusal to accept the passivity usually identified with America's elderly. The Panthers are not self-effacing. Deeply angry, they rock boats, not chairs.

However, the Panthers really are not violent. Despite their militancy, their tactics are an often unpredictable and eclectic mix including nonviolent action and demonstrations partly in the spirit of Martin Luther King, partly in the style of Saul Alinsky, but largely in the whimsical mode of their seventy-four-year-old national convener, Maggie Kuhn. The Panthers thus often charm those they attack.

For example, Maggie Kuhn and the San Francisco Panthers leafleted the 1977 national meeting of the Gerontological Society with four pages of questions including: "Is the profession of gerontology a parasite feeding on the expanding population of older people?"; "Does the Gerontological Society exist primarily to acquire research and training funds for universities and to advance the career goals of its members?" Yet the gerontologists eagerly attended the Panther's impromptu session, and some were in sympathy with Maggie Kuhn.

*Membership*

Although a large part of their membership is older persons, the Gray Panthers, despite their misleading name (originally coined by a reporter), emphasize that their slogan is "old and young in action." Indeed, Panthers resent being considered only of or for the old and define their mission more broadly as the creation of a better society for all ages. Although the intergenerational is stressed, Panther members are mainly either old or young—those who are retired or those not yet caught up in careers. While middle-aged Panthers are few, there is considerable leadership exercised by some hard-working women in their forties and fifties. Key midlife women include Alice Adler, a Chicago social worker, long-time activist, and chairperson of the thirty-person national steering committee. She arranged the first convention in 1975 in Chicago and founded the Chicago Panthers. Billie Heller, wife of a Beverly Hills producer, has a background with Nader's Raiders and helped organize seven or eight Panther chapters in Los Angeles, enrolling 700 members. Dr. Ellen Burns of the Catholic Social Service Center of Atlanta convened that city's interracial pack. A number of midlife nuns and ministers are also active Panthers.

*Activities*

Loosely organized and made up of essentially grass-roots participation except in the National Conventions that enable Panthers from diverse locales to meet, the Panthers' interests and activities are centered around the local or pack level.

The Washington, D.C. Panthers won a year's battle to stop the district from cutting 40,000 people off Medicare. Also they have organized tenants. Housing has been an issue for Panthers in other communities. One group was successful in getting public housing for the aged over tremendous resistance in an affluent suburb.

In 1977 Los Angeles Panthers focused attention on the lack of affordable housing by setting up a tent city on an elevated empty lot in view of the city hall and the *Los Angeles Times*. From their tent city, they sent delegates to the mayor's office, the city council, HUD, and elsewhere.

Greater Boston Panthers obtained a $15,000 grant to develop an inter-dependent living project for isolated persons. The New Jersey Panthers demonstrated against a pageant that they believed "exploited and infantilized" older persons. In Omaha, according to its report to the national convention, a "Panther on the prowl growled about public utilities" and represents consumers at board meetings of three utilities where "she's recognized as a knowledgable authority."

The Chicago Panthers sponsor an hour-and-a-half weekly radio program. The Kansas City Panthers won a lawsuit against a freeze on welfare funds. Cincinnati-area Panthers worked to get normal aging course content into schools. The San Diego Panthers, inspired by a twelve-year-old member, have fought for better food in school cafeterias.

An especially active Panther offshoot has been the Media Watch Task Force, first formed in 1974 in alliance with the Council on Interracial Books, which published a special issue, "Agism in Children's Books," in 1976. The Media Watch Committee, nicknamed the Watch Cats, is chaired by Lydia Bragger of New York City, who, with seven other volunteer monitors, has chided such people as Johnny Carson, Carol Burnett, Cher, Redd Foxx, and Dick Van Dyke for unfortunate portrayals of the elderly. This committee has attracted national attention, as evidenced by the fact that an article headlined "Gray Panthers Switched Off By TV," from a Long Island newspaper was placed in the U.S. Congressional Record.[2] The media committee raises consciousness about agism in many other ways, such as presenting a New York radio program.

Though local Panther chapters fight on various fronts to make "a better society for all," they carry the banner for the aged. In addition to a number of resolutions calling for general societal improvement, the 1977 National Convention itself passed specific resolutions on the aged. These included one enjoining the National Institute of Aging and Alcohol, Drug Abuse, and Mental Health Administration to correct the situation whereby older people are over-medicated rather than helped to deal with their real physical and emotional problems. Other resolutions called for departments of geriatric medicine in medical schools, better home health care, and the free expression of sexuality in old age.

Following their 1977 national convention, some Panthers demonstrated for their health concerns at the American Public Health Association meeting and for their consumer concerns by confering with Ralph Nader and picketing the U.S. Chamber of Commerce.

So Panthers do operate nationally and locally. The steering-committee members and Maggie Kuhn have testified on national legislation on such issues as full employment, long-term care, housing, national health care, mandatory retirement, food stamps, the B1 bomber, and a Senate bill on revision of the national criminal code. Nor are their activities only local and national; the Panthers have obtained a Non Government Organization seat with the office of Public Information of the United Nations. In 1976 several Panthers visited the People's Republic of China to observe the health-care system and treatment of the elderly.

## Maggie Kuhn and the Organization: Same or Different?

Forums and audiences are willing to hear and consider Maggie Kuhn's provocative statements precisely because of the disarming appearance, energy, and wit of this charismatic ninety-pound woman. Playing on contradictory stereotypes about old women, she manages to look grandmotherly, innocent, wise, and elfish simultaneously while admonishing her audience to "get off their asses." Her combination of radical ideology, demonstrated "straight" preretirement career, and personal power generate grass-roots Gray Panther packs convened by people who say, "I saw Maggie and I knew I had to do something." It is thus impossible to discuss the Gray Panthers, their activities, and their future as radical change agents without considering Maggie Kuhn.

Essentially because of Maggie Kuhn's charisma, national office manager Edith Giese and several others work for low wages in the tiny national Panther office in the basement of a Philadelphia church. In Maggie's home, which she shares with three young people in a largely black area of Philadelphia, Joanne Kernitz, her part-time secretary, labors to respond to all those contacting Maggie. Only in October 1979 did the Panthers begin to seek a full-time paid national coordinator.

No one, certainly not the Panthers themselves, dispute that Maggie created the Panthers and gave them national visibility. As the national treasurer observed at their 1977 convention, the Panthers lived for the first seven years "off Maggie's largesse." National Panther activities were funded largely by Maggie's honoraria. When the protective staff has suggested other Panthers as speakers to save Maggie's energy, the answer usually is "No, we want Maggie."

Like many other social movements, Panthers face the dilemma involved in depending on a mortal charismatic leader. Maggie's drive and enthusiasm are great; her physical health is not. Speaking and organizing across the country would exhaust anyone, especially one past seventy. Observers and Panther leaders wonder how much of the strength of the movement comes from Maggie's personal following and the loneliness of older Panthers and how much from the genuine discontent of those wanting radical social change. Maggie herself is acutely aware of this. Speaking at the 1977 convention evening of tribute to her, she said slowly, "Some of us will not be here at the next convention in two years." Accordingly she has begun to pay attention to the formal organization of the Panthers.

Although Maggie Kuhn had—in radical style of the 1960s—originally resisted development of a hierarchical structure or any particular set structure for the Panthers, by 1977 she had begun to attempt to turn the loose alliance of the members into a more formal organization that would have its own financial base and list of members. In the past the Panthers have been so flexible as a movement that no one knows exactly how many Panthers there are. National officers estimate that there are about 100 grass-roots networks around the country and perhaps less than 10,000 Panthers affiliated in groups or as individuals. Over the years so many have requested the *Network* (the national Panther newspaper tie-line and forum) that the list was pared in 1977 for financial reasons from 10,000 to the 4,500 sending individual or organizational subscription fees; and a seventy-six-year-old volunteer does all newspaper mailings.

Nor have the Panthers traditionally collected dues. Only at the 1977 convention, seven years after the Panthers started, was it decided to consider national dues, and the steering committee was empowered to develop a dues structure. More resources were vital. For example, the one national headquarters telephone line was always busy. Selling Panther T-shirts and literature was inadequate. Expecting opposition, leaders suggested dues hesitantly to members assembled at the convention. But Panthers voted unanimously for them, though many people stressed that some people are too poor to pay, and, in appropriate radical tradition, a motion was passed that no one should be exempted from membership who could not afford dues. However, on the whole, as one woman who urged that dues be required commented, "Panthers feel it is chintzy not to have them."

Establishing the principle of dues signals a marked organizational change from the free-wheeling individualism formerly characteristic of the movement. Up until this point, anyone who inquired about Panthers received a form letter, which said in part:

> We are glad for your interest in the Gray Panther Movement. We are a coalition of young and old people advocating social change for the social justice and human liberation of all people. We hope that you concur with the Articles of Agreement adopted by the National Steering Committee as the basis for affiliation and united action.
>
> The process for individual affiliation is detailed in Article III and is as follows:
>
> a.  Any individual who is in agreement with and willing to work toward the Gray Panther purpose and goals may become affiliated by submitting written agreement with the purpose and goals.
> b.  Each affiliate is requested to make an annual contribution to the Gray Panthers.

Thus, although inquirers were asked for contribution, the Panther appeal is largely to those with little money to spare—older persons on fixed income and young persons not earning much. While in 1977 the Panthers hoped to get $47,000 they took in only $42,000. The paid workers from the national office who came to the convention were owed back wages until a bowl was passed to raise funds, yielding $1457 from about 300 Panthers. It was a small amount indeed, but it represented financial sacrifice for many with limited incomes and no expense accounts.

To raise money outside the membership, the Panthers have taken two steps. They engaged a firm that solicits contributions for a variety of social-service groups. Also, the Panthers hired a part-time worker at the usual semi-volunteer wage, to solicit foundations and the government. This latter step to hire a paid fund-raiser was made with considerable debate and anxiety. Some Panthers have expressed fear that taking money from foundations supported by industry or government will limit their freedom. The paradox of the organization, however, is that the $16,000 granted by the Administration on Aging (AoA) of the Department of Health, Education and Welfare for the 1977 convention did not inhibit Maggie from telling Panthers from the podium that she had been rereading conflict theorists such as Marx and finding good ideas. She pointed out carefully, however, "I am not a Communist." Nor did AoA funding stop Panthers from passing resolutions critical of federal agencies.

Interestingly the AoA grant was used to bring Panthers who could not otherwise have come to the conference. The Boston chapter, for example, used its portion of this grant so a Panther from a nursing home could attend. It is ironic that the Panther's first grant in 1970 was antiestablishment—$1,000 from the People's Fund, which was largely supported by students critical of the government's Vietnam policy.

**The Search for Structure and Ideology**

To add structure as well as better financing, in 1978 the Panthers regionalized into four coordinating areas. This regional leadership works with a thirty-person National Steering Committee. In addition caucuses formed at the 1977 convention of Panthers in the various states or geographic areas, like New England. (Until the 1977 convention, some did not know what nearby groups were doing.) Another indication of greater organizational control was evident in 1977 when delegates voted that persons should not speak without formal authorization. There was also talk of making packs more structured. Not surprisingly, not all attendees agreed. Splits in most radical social movements are inevitable parts of solidification of organizational means and goals. For example, at the 1977 convention the issue generating the most heat and consuming the most time was a possible position paper entitled *Economic Rights— Economic Democracy*. What happened to this radical critique of the free enterprise system may be prognostic of how the Panthers may evolve as they broaden membership. This twelve-page document was included in the registration packets, and Panthers were asked to read it prior to the session of the convention where it was the main item on the agenda. Some Panthers who had been active in left circles all their lives were enthusiastic about this document and urged that it become part of the Panther principles.

However, other Panthers, especially newer recruits, were upset. Their resistance was epitomized by a man who took the floor to explain: "My father and grandfather helped found the Farm Labor Party in Minnesota. I came to the Panthers and this convention in good faith. This is a little too sudden for me. Can you give us rookies as Gray Panthers some consideration? I want to put my new Panther network into operation but this item is too much for me.

I am against such things as public ownership of transportation. You are going a little too fast for me."

Maggie responded, "Thank you for your comment. May I say we are constantly educating ourselves. I hope we will educate you tonight in the discussion."

Panthers then lined up at the floor microphone to urge passionately for or against the paper. It became apparent that acceptance of the document might result in some Panthers leaving. This would have been a replay of their 1975 convention when some walked out after the vote favoring legalization of marijuana. One Panther became so worried that the measure would pass and so would destroy the Panthers that she asked Maggie to "cool the issue" and prevent passage. Maggie, who was seated on the convention floor, replied she thought the three Panthers on the platform could handle the situation and that she trusted the Panthers.

That Kuhn is the Panthers as well as of the Panthers is demonstrated by this ideological and personal interplay. Advocates of the economic paper soon withdrew their motion for its passage when they saw the schism that she had highlighted but refused to solve. By withdrawing their motion the radicals clearly showed that the solidarity of the Panthers was more important to them than pushing socialist ideology.

## What Is the Future and the Impact?

As retired minister Cameron Hall, who helped found the Panthers, said, "Maggie has created a national movement in only seven years, and this is an achievement on par with the creation of the National Council of Mental Health and the National Conference of Christians and Jews."

It remains to be seen whether the Panthers merit Michael Harrington's 1977 convention accolade to them: "The movement you represent is one of the most important and dynamic movements that has ever come. Your movement is not a movement apart but is a movement relating to many other constituencies."

Harrington's description is a hope that Maggie and the Panthers share. Is it a reality? Are the Panthers an intergenerational movement for overall social change that will have a substantial impact? Or are they simply part of the diverse members of the aged's lobby—headlined by the *New York Times* on 24 October 1977 as "Gray Power Getting Results in Congress?"

To be widely effective the Panthers must develop a wider membership base. They are deeply aware of the fact that they are predominantly too middle class, too white, and too intellectual. One retired blue-collar union Panther complained publicly at the 1977 convention because "the literature is so high-faluting, I can't read it."

At the 1977 convention where enthusiastic Panthers were sought after by many media people, one had the feeling Panthers were indeed powerful.

In the communities Panthers are resourceful at holding creative demonstrations that the media love. What gerontologist Robert Binstock suggested at the 1977 convention as a plan of action—make a nuisance of yourselves—they know how to do with superb flair.

However, if one surveys older persons, one often finds that many have not heard of the Gray Panthers. If one questions the general public of all ages about the Panthers, one often gets blank stares or the response, "Do you mean the *Black* Panthers?"

The Panthers have their fans and are growing, although they do not now have the membership or apparatus of such entrenched, less controversial organizations as the American Association of Retired Persons and the National Council of Senior Citizens. Some of these organizations view the Panthers anxiously. Frank Manning, the seventy-eight-year-old leader of the influential Massachusetts Association of Older Americans, was asked about the Panthers at his group's 1977 fall meeting. Usually voluble, Manning answered a member's question from the floor with brevity: "We welcome the cooperation of the Gray Panthers. We should be able to get together on what affects the elderly though we disagree on philosophy. Next question."

The question for the Panthers is what will happen in the next few years. As noted earlier, Maggie is worried about this. Here are some things she told the 1977 conventioneers at various times during the four-day meeting. "We have a lot of work to do and not too long to do it. Panthers multiply. . . . For many people, young and old, there is an intense personal awareness and not social awareness and this is confining. . . . We must work for our radicalization. . . . The first step in organizing is to change ourselves but this can't be secured apart from basic changes in society."

Maggie, the founder of the movement, is probably its best critic. In her concluding remarks to the convention she said:

> We have gathered strength and wider social awareness for the long road ahead. We must develop new and creative ways to work in the networks for grass-root support to test in small do-able actions. We have to organize on a twenty-four-hour basis to keep us alive and at it. I am terribly glad the young caucus met and hope there will be renewed commitment by young people and that we will always be advocates of the liberation of young people in our society.
>
> The media attempts to push us into caring only for old folks. We have to close ranks; agism oppresses us all. We have to use the media instead of the media using us and not be seduced by it.
>
> We have received a large measure of popularity and we have to resist the temptation to be on ego trips or to have power. But we must be faithful to our goals. . . . We can have community. . . . We have to go forward and recognize honest differences in philosophy and strategy. Controversy is all right, but we must not be divided. To be in turmoil is not appropriate and takes up too much energy.

There have been marvelous people burned out, and we have to refresh ourselves and have a live, loving community which enhances Gray Panthers. . . . My love to each of you, and I ask each of you to be my kindly frank critics. Look to each other to keep us on the track; be honest and carry forward with the integrity our movement requires. There is not too much love or integrity in the world. We must be kindly disposed to each other.

Gray Panthers are on a long pilgrimage, a long hard march, and never forget we are on a pilgrimage but also on a lark.

Maggie sets a high standard for herself and the Panthers. Will the young Panthers stay committed as they acquire middle-aged responsibilities? Can Panthers recruit more middle-aged persons who have more to lose than the elderly? Will the new breed of conservative youth join?

Will additional old people be wooed by Panthers away from isolation or the more conservative service-offering and benefit-seeking elderly groups? Some of these groups may adopt some outward trappings of the Panthers without their radical critique. In fact the Panthers claim they have affected the traditional senior groups. Maggie says that as a result of their emphasis on youth and age in action, the American Association of Retired Persons has begun to court youth.

Will the Panthers prosper or grow only to dilute their fervor and mission in order to get funds or keep harmony? Will grants, as feared, bring a muzzling? Maggie has warned the Panthers to choose their friends carefully, recognizing the Panthers may be co-opted and used. (It was, after all, easier for the Administration on Aging to give the Panthers $16,000 for a convention than for AoA to change medicine, housing, or the nursing-home industry.)

The Panthers know that they are at an important turning point. The steering committee sent conventioneers home with a questionnaire for responses to this statement: "All issues involving agism are of concern to the Gray Panthers but the Gray Panthers as a national movement has to set priorities. In your opinion, what should be the primary goal now and in the near future. . . . How can this union across the generations be strengthened to effect social change?"

An important tension for the Panthers is the balance between the personal concerns of some older Panthers and the general social critique. While Maggie Kuhn has repeatedly stated that if the elderly are just for themselves they have lost everything, some believe the Panthers should concentrate their power on helping the elderly. This point was emphasized by Michael Harrington who, at the 1977 convention, warned, "Don't dissolve into an amorphous coalition. I think older people need an organization concerned with their specific problems. I think it extremely important for this movement to fight to get treatable diseases treated and end custodial mentality and to get the money so people do not have to die before they should."

However, Harrington, like the Panthers, was ambivalent. Later he told the Panthers to work against military production and for full employment—hardly "gray" issues—saying that the fate of the old depended on full employment for without it there would be intergenerational war. Thus the Panthers and their friends expect concentration on their mission for the old but also action on other issues—a very large job.

Panthers face real possibilities and dangers. Ten years ago no one could have predicted that high honoraria would be paid an older woman largely unknown outside of Presbyterian Church circles until her forced retirement. The activist students who helped Maggie at the beginning and continue to do so probably could not have shared such a movement without the fight against the Vietnam war or Maggie's charisma. Who can predict now what will happen to the Panthers in the long run? *The San Francisco Examiner* on 29 April 1977 headlined an article "Mightie Maggie's Just Begun." Maggie herself has changed to accept more organization and structure. A successor to her might take the movement in a different direction.

Though Maggie's skills and talent are rare, a number of other older persons have developed self-confidence and become prominent Panthers. Anne Binyon of Chicago, a former teacher, is often described as the Maggie Kuhn of the Midwest. She acts in the Free Street Two Theater of Chicago made up entirely of those over sixty-five and speaks at times when Maggie is speaking elsewhere. Lois Harris of the Boston Panthers, a Quaker now studying at Pendle Hill, is another possible successor. Still another is Lillian Rabinowitz of Berkeley. There are many others in the movement that give old and young people acceptance, a chance to matter, and strategies.

It is impossible to predict what will happen to the Panthers eventually. Most movements fade when their original leaders go; others regenerate. There is the danger that Panthers will be caught in the backlash against the aged and young as the middle-aged struggle to survive ever-rising taxes and compete for scarce employment and resources. Thus there is the possibility that Gray Panthers may join the many transient radical American movements that fought and lost.

No matter what happens in the long run, it is likely that within the near future the group will continue to act as a catalyst to some old and young who will be moved to shake up bureaucrats and legislators nationally and locally. In the process Panthers will provide diversion and entertainment for observers and much social integration, support, and expression for their members.

Above all, Panthers will not let agism go uncriticized and they will not settle for arts and crafts, hot lunches, or paternalism to the aged or the young. By their obtrusive and continuous presence they may indeed contribute to social consciousness about the deficiencies in American social structure and values. If nothing else, they have changed the image of the old from pushover pussy cats to feisty prowling Panthers.

**Post Script**

This chapter was completed before the 1979 Gray Panther Training Conference and Third Biennial Convention was held on 25 to 28 October in Chevy Chase,

Maryland. After careful review of the resolutions passed at this convention, Dr. Jacobs felt that the thrust of the 1979 resolutions paralleled those of the 1977 meeting. She noted no significant indication of change in the philosophy reported in her essay.

The 1979 resolutions covered a considerable array of issues and are consonant with the intergenerational character and philosophy of the organization. Gray Panther members comprise a wide range of ages, and their concerns are reflected in such areas as consumer advocacy, women and federal pensions, nursing homes, nuclear weapons, pollution, and dental care.

The current direction of the Gray Panthers is discernible in resolutions addressing:

Abortion: The constitutional right of women to freedom of choice is affirmed;

Taxes: The alleviation of tax burdens should not be at the expense of minorities and the poor. Sales tax, value-added tax, and legislation like California's Proposition 13 are opposed;

Military spending: The Gray Panthers resolved to cooperate with other groups to plan a national strategy to inform the public about the extent of military spending and the need to convert that spending to human needs;

Pensions: The convention recognized that people are often ignorant of the unpleasant economic realities of pensions and Social Security and consequently retire into a condition of poverty. The resolution includes attaining secure and adequate income for older Americans, publicizing the plight of pension losers and advocating their right to a decent life. The Panthers also favor federal legislation to make it possible for older people to work as long as they are willing and able to do so, with no upper age limit or economic restrictions.[3]

Editors

## Notes

1. See, for example, Matilda White Riley and Anne Foner, *Aging and Society*, vol. 1 (New York: Russell Sage, 1968); Beth B. Hess and Elizabeth W. Markson, *Aging and Old Age* (New York: Macmillan, 1980).

2. U.S., Congress, 2nd Session Senate, *Congressional Record*, vol. 122, no. 11, February 2, 1976.

3. *Gray Panther Network*, November/December 1979, pp. A and C of Special Insert, "New Resolutions and Articles."

# 8

# Institutionalization: Sin, Cure, or Sinecure for the Impaired Elderly

*Elizabeth W. Markson*

"Nursing Home A Firetrap, Local Official Says"; "Overbilling Revealed at Institution"; "Gang Visits by Physicians at Shady Acres Charged"; "Old People Found Lying in Filth at Nursing Home." These fictitious headlines are based on recent factual media reports about institutions for the elderly. Institutional care for the frail and infirm old, while increasingly an integral part of the American system of health care, has also been under attack. There is probably no large urban area in the United States that has not had at least one nursing-home scandal within the past few years. The growth of nursing homes has been viewed by some as a manifestation of the breakdown of family ties as well as other social sins or departures from tried and true ways, and the congregate care institution itself has been criticized as providing a sinecure for greedy owners and a haven for untrained, often uncaring, workers. Less has been claimed about the nursing home or other old-age institution as a curing facility, although proponents of long-term care argue that treatment received at such a place is necessary, palliative, and rehabilitative.

As we grapple with the issue of what comprises suitable care for the frail and handicapped old, we are prone to view the topic as uniquely American, associated with our own peculiar social and cultural history. Yet despite different national histories, cultural values, and social institutions, most contemporary industrialized countries face similar problems in the organization, financing, and delivery of care to those old people who, for a variety of reasons, cannot take care of themselves. For example, although the Australian Constitution, unlike those of the United States and Canada, specifically recognizes governmental power to legislate for age and invalid pensions, and an Invalid and Old Age Act was passed in 1908, in 1974 the Social Welfare Commission of the Australian Government reported:

> . . . present housing and care provisions for aged and handicapped people consist of a patchwork of services which have grown up on an inadequately planned basis both in the overall balance of services provided and in the particular regions and localities in which they are distributed. While parts of these programs are adequate the services are often unsatisfactory because of these gaps in the present provisions and also division in jurisdictions, the methods of funding, and legislative regulations.[1]

Early recognition of a problem area does not guarantee resolution.

That institutional care for the aged has gained salience as a current social issue in the United States and elsewhere is a reflection of the changing demographic composition of the population of contemporary industrialized nations. Until relatively recently old people in institutions and institutional facilities designed primarily for the old were rare. Until the twentieth century, relatively few people lived until they were old; those who did were likely to be both economically well off and physically healthy.[2] In the United States in 1910, there were only about 80,000 people sixty-five and over in institutions of any kind. By 1978 there were about 1.3 million old people residing in nursing homes, old-age homes, long-term-care hospitals, and mental hospitals.

The enhanced life expectancy that has occurred over the past seventy years is closely related to decline in acute and infectious diseases as leading causes of death, a decline largely due to rise in real income and standard of living;[3] improvement in public health and hygiene standards, and, to a much lesser extent, immunization and medical therapy.[4] Paradoxically, although the average life expectancy at birth has changed dramatically, the life span has not. The celebrated longevity of Old Testament heroes and that of contemporary people in portions of the USSR is more the result of inaccurate recordkeeping, different ways of counting years, and faulty recollection than of verified fact.[5] Eating yogurt and exercising indeed may make one feel well but do not alter the life span. Nor is there any solid evidence that the life span of people has changed since ancient times. What has changed are the proportions of people who survive to old age and the causes of death for the population from acute to chronic diseases.

**Is Institutional Care New?**

Despite the increase in the number of old people in the population, long-term institutionalization of the elderly is not a new modality of care. In the United States it may be traced to the Elizabethan Poor Law, passed in England in 1601, which laid the ground for much subsequent welfare legislation in the United States and England. This legislation, distinguishing the aged, the impotent poor, and children from the able-bodied poor, provided for the former group in an almshouse or poorhouse where custodial care was supplied under the supervision of the municipality. While the social conditions and attitudes to which the destitute aged, infirm, and children inmates were subjected were less than ideal, the almshouse did permit economy of scale and close supervision of the 'moral worth' of those receiving sustenance. Many of the same conditions of the almshouse have persisted to the present day in old-age facilities. For example, the practice of separating husband and wife on admission and the lack of individuation of treatment and scheduling of activities continue in many contemporary old-age institutions.

What the almshouse provided was a relatively inexpensive and safe facility in which the destitute and infirm might be isolated. Early medical hospitals, too, fulfilled this dual social control and care function. Benjamin Franklin, describing the need for a public hospital in Philadelphia, argued that this facility would provide a spot in which those who tended to wander aimlessly and frighten their neighbors or had lost their senses might be confined. He also advocated care for the sick in one central location as a cheaper modality than sending aid to their homes—a persisting idea in delivery of care in contemporary society. Finally, continued Franklin, establishment of the hospital for care of the indigent of all ages serves the additional function of relieving the middle class from the unpleasant task of seeing the poor die in the streets.[6]

If the undifferentiated almshouse and hospitals for the poor developed in the seventeenth century, where were the families of these people? We all know that the number of old people in nursing homes and other long-term-care facilities is due to the dereliction of duty by the family, death of the extended family during the last fifty years, and increasing urbanization—or do we? Historical evidence suggests that this popular formulation is over-simplified. Neither industrialization nor modernization are events peculiar to the twentieth century; rather, they took place over several centuries during which the social and economic functions of the family have gradually changed and contracted.[7] With the disintegration of the feudal state, the family or clan declined as the base for political and economic power. The increased mobility of people moving from defunct or dwindling feudal estates to cities to seek work contributed to the rise of the metropolis and development of the nuclear family structure now current in contemporary industrialized societies. In lieu of hereditary social and economic position, characteristic of the feudal monarchy, capitalism emerged, distinguished by task specialization, division of labor, and impersonality. With the rise of capitalism came added emphasis on market relationships rather than on traditional personalized master-serf and familial-clan ties. As the individual person achieved more freedom and became more able to make choices that were not immutably fixed by family traditions and ritual, the family as the cornerstone for political, economic, and social organization declined. One's position in the economic structure rather than place in the family thus became a significant indicator of life chances and status as well as life style.

According to recent evidence uncovered by Lazlett and Chambers, the extended family as the most common type of family structure in England was defunct by the seventeenth century.[8] Rather than remaining with one set of parents, the young husband-wife pair generally created a new household; married sons did not remain in their parental homes. Unless there were unmarried adult children, parents lived alone in their own homes. Many old people lived as boarders with nonkin or alone. Increased specialization of jobs and the factory system of the industrial revolution further aided the development of the nuclear family. The ability of young people to find their own jobs freed them more and more from the power and authority of parents and encouraged establish-ment of a household physically, economically, and socially separate from that of one's parents or older siblings.

It was precisely such gradual changes as these that led to the passage of the Elizabethan Poor Law in the seventeenth century and laid the ground for later social welfare and health legislation in Britain. Large numbers of old people were relatively unaffected. Since their number was few, no special concern was given to their care. The economically self-sufficient elderly lived as they chose, and the indigent old were placed in an almshouse or public hos-pital. A similar pattern developed in American society where the extended family was never the norm. In the United States, patterns of power and social and economic organization transplanted from England, coupled with the access-ibility of new lands and jobs in the new world, made the extended family the exception rather than the rule. Nor did the expanding frontier favor develop-ment of an extended family. In a country where the relatively tradition-free norms of exploration, expansion, and exploitation of new territories were honored, the tight structure and spatially bound locus of an extended family was impractical.

An exception to this is the pattern of family structure brought by Eastern and Southern European immigrants and by the Irish in the nineteenth and early twentieth centuries. Because of the particular cultures and expectations brought with them, many of these people anticipated and expected that their American-born children would be responsible for their care in old age. This may have given rise to the current myth of the prevalence of the extended family in the United States.

As more and more people survive to old age, we have not developed many new ways of caring for them. Instead services based on a very old model have been expanded and improved.

### Are Institutions Necessarily Bad?

Congregate-care facilities for the aged are total institutions where diverse human needs are handled by a bureaucratic organization promoting group living rather than attention to individual needs and wants.[9] As used by sociologist Erving Goffman, a *total institution* is a facility in which the usual barriers separating work, leisure, and sleeping locales are abandoned. Instead of segmentation of these three facets of life, the total institution provides for carrying out all aspects of life in the same place and under the same authority.[10] Batch living, too, characterizes the total institution. People are required to do the same things together, and there is little or no opportunity for privacy and autonomy of activity.[11] The activities are tightly scheduled and designed to fit the plans of the institution. They are imposed with an official purpose.[12]

Total institutions may be categorized according to their purpose. Nursing homes, homes for the elderly, poor, and infirm are all designed to care for people perceived to be harmless and incompetent; mental hospitals contain persons who are incompetent but may be harmful to themselves or others. Jails, boarding schools, camps, colleges, armies, and monasteries are also total institutions. The common denominator of all these facilities is that they are essentially resocializing institutions designed to change people and their feelings about themselves.[13] Total institutions need not have negative effects. Rather, the term delineates an underlying structural design. However, the majority of data about institutional care for old people indicates that the total institution is less than an ideal solution since change is often negative rather than positive.

About a quarter of a century ago, investigators began to comment on the poorer social, psychological, and physical functioning of nursing-home residents and suggested that a constellation of factors, including poor adjustment prior to institutionalization, may be the cause of the worsened state of residents.[14] More recent work, such as that by Tobin and Lieberman expands on this thesis, suggesting that much of the negative portrait of the elderly institutionalized person may be due to preadmission effects, relocation, and the process of selection as well as the totality of the institution.[15] Data from the National Nursing Home Survey for 1977 (the most recent year for which material has been analyzed) indicates that 54.2 percent of the residents in nursing homes were admitted from another hospital or health facility, most often a general hospital.[16] Only 13.5 percent of the men and 7.9 percent of the women residents in nursing homes are not dependent in any dimension of self-care.[17] These bits of information lend credence to the claim that the poor condition of nursing home residents is due at least in part to their illness or incapacity at admission.

Yet it is generally agreed that successful aging is more likely to occur when there is relatively little discontinuity of life patterns between late maturity and old age. Some of the negative effects of institutional care reported among the old no doubt occur because ties with their familiar worlds and existing role relationships are broken, and a new kind of institutionally appropriate behavior must be learned. Yet the majority of institutions offer the patient relatively little. The basic requirements for adult socialization—that new values and behaviors be inculcated—are not met. Instead residents are required only to accept medical and nursing care passively. According to the 1977 National Nursing Home Survey, 68.6 percent of the patients in nursing homes did not participate in any activity outside the facility within the last month, and only 10.6 percent took an overnight leave from the institution within the last year.[18] Further evidence for the lack of stimulation within the nursing-home environment is provided by a study of forty nursing homes in which residents were observed during twenty-four one-hour segments. More than one half of the residents' time was spent doing nothing.[19] Nor were contacts between staff members and residents the norm; fewer than one in four old people received any nursing-staff contact.[20] In the nursing home or other long-term-care facility, time is passed rather than put toward some well-delineated goal as in an active treatment or resocializing institution. National data indicate that in 1977 no discharge was planned or anticipated for 96.2 percent of nursing-home residents. Only 35 percent of the residents received any therapy service (including physical, recreational, occupational, or speech or hearing therapy, counseling, reality orientation, or other therapy service) within the last month.[21] Therapeutic inactivity with the expectation of visits by physicians—about 65 percent had seen a physician within the last month—is the norm.[22]

How good is the care provided in nursing homes for the aged? The answer is that it varies immensely. One of the most outspoken critics of the nursing-home industry, Mendelson, has criticized proprietary homes on the grounds that they are ridden with "high profits and patient abuse, with government as a silent accomplice."[23] Concealed ownership, where the operator of the nursing home is identified but the owner is not, has, she suggested, enabled kickbacks and income-tax evasion. Other abuses include cutting costs of patient care in order to make a profit, kickbacks to pharmacies, overdrugging of patients, "gang visits" by a physician who "dashes through the nursing home in a couple of hours, then bills Medicaid for sixty or seventy-five or ninety patient visits,"[24] performance of unnecessary services, and overbilling by dentists, physicians, optometrists, pharmacists, and other providers of services to nursing-home patients. While government is reponsible for inspection and certification of nursing homes for Medicare and Medicaid, "all of these procedures take time, and the process can be turned off at any of the stages."[25] Inspection has been lax and ineffective in a system that is conducive to bribery at all levels.

While a variety of studies have examined the relationship between types of ownership of the institution and level of care,[26] no clear findings have emerged. Rather, quality of the facility is affected by the source of payment, the institution itself, and sociocultural patterns. Some proprietary homes are excellent, others are very bad. Similarly some non-profit and government-owned facilities are outstanding; others are not. Each has its economic problems of abuse and corruption.

Whether institutional care is appropriate to all those who are currently receiving it is another topical issue, although most data on this are fragmentary or represent guesstimates. Mendelson has presented data indicating that 29 percent of patients in Michigan nursing homes did not require skilled nursing care, and in New York City between 53 percent and 61 percent of the Medicaid patients surveyed did not need to be in nursing homes.[27] Testimony at the House Select Committee on Aging in 1977 indicated that an estimated 15 to 20 percent of the individuals in nursing homes in Texas do not require such care.[28]

Overutilization by the elderly has been noted in mental hospitals as well. In New York City over one third of the old people in two mental hospitals were judged to be able to return to the community if there were group homes, a day-care center, or some extended supervision in the home available. Interestingly another third were judged suitable for nursing-home care because they had minimal psychiatric symptoms and their physical conditions required nursing care.[29]

Nor has increased funding led to improved care. While considerable governmental and private allocations of money and manpower have been channeled into institutional care of the elderly in hospitals, nursing homes, personal care homes, and homes for the aged, thus far no payment plan has proved to be a panacea in old age. Shulman and Galanter observed that "the nursing home industry is a disaster, well documented by innumerable investigations and reports."[30] Recent congressional hearings indicated that some personal care or adult homes may be dangerous and inappropriate.[31] The mental hospital, too, has been scored as "expensive, inefficient, frequently anti-therapeutic, and never the treatment of choice."[32] To what extent are these criticisms valid? Before examining the processes and effects of institutional care, it is important to consider several broader social issues relating to institutionalization and being old in America.

### Agism and Loss of Role

In American society worth or social standing has been traditionally assigned to men on the basis of their real or apparent social and economic contribution and achievement of which education, occupation, and wealth are the most common indices. In the case of women, the status of father and husband traditionally determined social status. Furthermore the United States is an activist society where work is valued as an end in itself. Belief in the "goodness" of action and the "badness" of inaction runs deep. Only recently have love and leisure been considered as legitimate pursuits as work. Death, sine qua non of inactivity and cessation of achievement, remains an unwelcome and dreaded confrontation. The elderly lose on both counts; not only are they less active than the young but they are the age group most likely to die.

Put another way, if social value is measured by productive capacity, the worth of the old and retired person is low. Nor is it that their production is needed in our society. Sociologist Irving Rosow observed that "The aged are a problem precisely because the United States is such an affluent society."[33] The labor of old people is not needed. Despite recession, the United States is too wealthy and younger individuals too self-sufficient to need the old either as workers or sources of tradition. The lack of a significant socially productive role for the elderly combined with their greater frailty has led to conceptualization of old age as a social and medical problem, preferably one amenable to corrective or palliative treatment. Yet, despite passage of Medicare, old age is accorded lower social value than youth. The elderly still tend to receive less care and consideration when they become handicapped or ill. Alex Comfort's statement is relevant: "One wonders what Archie Bunker would feel about immigrants if he knew that on his sixty-fifth birthday he would turn into a Puerto Rican. White racists don't turn black, black racists don't become white, male chauvinists don't become women, anti-Semites don't wake up and find themselves Jewish—but we have a lifetime of indoctrination with the idea of the difference and inferiority of the old."[34]

In illness, the older person with heart disease, cancer, or another major disease is less likely to receive the same sort of intensive care for as long a period as a younger person. The appropriateness of heroics in treatment for any age group is a subject of controversy. Suffice it to say that the old person is more likely than the young to be transferred to an extended or long-term-care facility whenever possible (Medicare provides for 100 days of such benefits for people sixty-five years old and over), thereby freeing up a bed in the short-term, active treatment hospital where younger patients are more likely to be treated.[35]

## Social Class and Income

In addition to age, social class (a crude indicator of which is income) is critical in determining the kind of care one will receive. For example, while Medicare is based on the premise that medical care should be available to all social-security recipients on a nondiscriminatory basis, a recent analysis of Medicare payments by Karen Davis showed that benefits are not distributed equally among income classes.[36] Old people with incomes above $15,000 per year received 45 percent more days of hospital care on the average than did lower income persons with similar health conditions, and they received twice the payments for physician and other services. In addition the average reimbursement for each physician visit was 50 percent higher among the high-income as compared to low-income people. This suggests, in part, a tendency among higher income elderly to receive higher quality and more specialized services. Wildavsky has dubbed this the "axiom of inequality," where "the wealthier aged, who can afford to pay, receive not merely the same benefits as the aged poor but even more, because they are better able to negotiate the system. Class tells."[37]

The elderly of low social status are also likely to be placed in a 'deprived institution,' such as the mental hospital.[38] In a study of 348 referrals to two state mental hospitals serving the New York City area, 86 percent of those elderly referred for inpatient care as compared to 59 percent of the general population sixty-five and over had not gone beyond elementary school; their occupational status paralleled their low educational status and 77.7 percent were at the bottom of the occupational scale.[39]

## Race and Ethnicity

Both race and ethnicity are salient factors influencing the kind and quality of care received in old age. Manard et al. noted an inverse relationship between the proportion of nonwhite elderly in the general population and the proportion in old age institutions; that is, states with large nonwhite populations are generally characterized by low institutional rates in such facilities.[40] Much of this is associated with discriminatory practices in admission and utilization of different types of facilities.

Elderly blacks are disproportionately represented in state mental hospitals (which are not old-age institutions per se, although about 30 percent of their inmates are sixty-five and over), whites predominate in nursing and old-age homes.[41] For the black old, the problem is not one of keeping out of an institution but of receiving appropriate care when required.[42]

Various hypotheses about the low rates of nursing and old-age home utilization among nonwhites have been proposed that complement the discriminatory practices of some facilities. These include a concentration of nonwhite elderly in geographic areas that have low institutional rates in general as well as a low representation of elderly in the total population.[43] Nonwhites have lower life expectancies than whites in our society, so that few very old nonwhites survive to be institutionalized.[44] Poverty, too, is important. Despite the passage of Medicare and Medicaid, states with a high proportion of very poor aged tend to have low rates of nursing-home use. No doubt this reflects the relative wealth of these states themselves. The major growth has been proprietary, or profit-making, long-term facilities; these are most likely to develop in relatively affluent areas where there is capital to invest. In areas short of such institutions, admission preference is probably given to the relatively well-off old; the poor, minority members, and other less socially valued people are screened out. Finally, old minority women are more likely to live with their children and grandchildren where they act as babysitters, housekeepers, and the like. When they become ill or frail, they have resources within their household on which to rely for social support and physical care until their situation becomes impossible.

For the white ethnic aged, the rationale for institutionalization is somewhat different. The foreign-born elderly differ from the foreign born in the general population. First of all there are more of them. In 1970, for example, 15 percent of those sixty-five and over were foreign born as compared to 5 percent of the U.S. general population. The old foreign born are more likely to reside in the Northeastern United States and to have come from Eastern or Southern Europe than are younger ethnics. Poverty, low socioeconomic status, and foreign birth compound the probability of being institutionalized in a mental hospital.

Data for New York City indicate that not only are the foreign born old overrepresented (59 percent compared to 43 percent in the population sixty-five and over), but those who receive institutional care are most likely to come from Eastern and Southern Europe, the ethnic groups most successful since immigration.[45] In 1952 the highest family incomes were found among those of Russian, Polish, and Italian extraction—$13,929, $12,182, and $11,646 respectively—in comparison to the median family income for all Americans regardless of origin, which was about $11,000.[46] This may well be due to the social costs of upward mobility. While those ethnic old most likely to be institutionalized are people who have been advantaged enough to survive to old age, they have nonetheless failed to move up in the class structure themselves. Their children, however, have fulfilled the American Dream. The changing nature of the white ethnic family is also relevant. While the first generation of an ethnic family may be very tightly knit, the second generation has been expected to succeed in the majority culture and retain strong ties with their heritage. Choices must be made; often upward mobility can be won only at the price of rejection of parts of one's ethnic background.

## Sex

At age seventy, the average American woman can expect to live 13.6 more years, the man 10.5 years. Because of these sex differences in life expectancy, as women grow older they are likely to find themselves in the company of other women or alone. To be white, female, middle class—all factors enhancing life expectancy—living alone and having one or more physical disabilities increases the likelihood of entering a nursing home.

In 1977, 71.2 percent of nursing-home residents were women as compared to 28.8 percent who were men.[47] Women were obviously overrepresented in these facilities in comparison to their numbers in the general population. Despite their greater preponderance, the reasons for which women are admitted do not differ appreciably from those for men.

Most likely to be admitted to a nursing home are people of either sex who are widowed or never married. Since most women can expect to outlive their spouses, it is not surprising that elderly widows predominate in nursing homes.

## Living Arrangements Prior to Admission

Contrary to popular belief, most old people in nursing homes are not sent there from their children's homes. Somewhat more than half (54.2 percent of people in nursing homes in 1977) were admitted from another hospital or health facility, most often the general hospital (32.3 percent) or another nursing home (12.5 percent). An additional 13.7 percent were living alone at home, 5.6 percent were living with a spouse, and 28.8 percent were living with other persons. Only slightly over 10 percent were living with their children.[48]

It is, however, one's children who are most likely to arrange for admission to a nursing home, most often because there are no community resources known or readily available to care for the aging relative. In 1977, 39.1 percent of the residents of nursing homes had had their admission arranged by their children, 19.8 percent had had their care arranged by other relatives, and slightly over 5 percent of the residents arranged for their own admission, a figure similar to the proportion of people whose spouse arranged for their care (5.8 percent). The remainder of residents had their nursing-home care arranged by a variety of other agents, including hospital and social-service agencies. It is clear that the nursing home is being used as a facility to care for those people who, for a variety of reasons, have inadequate social supports or resources that provide community alternatives.

## Some Unresolved Issues in the Quality of Long-Term Care

Although the graying of America receives considerable attention now, interest in the process of aging and the special health needs of the old was confined to a few scholars at a relatively small number of institutions until the last two decades. Gerontology and geriatrics today remain relatively underdeveloped and unpopular topics among those entering the health-care field, and, as the Institute of Medicine of the National Academy of Sciences pointed out in 1978, interest in the elderly tends to diminish over the four-year period of medical education. Contributory factors include agism, reinforcement of negative attitudes by faculty and resident physicians, lack of excitement about the chronicity of many of the health problems of the aged, and incomplete or inappropriate knowledge of desirable services and possible structures for delivery of services to various target groups of the elderly including the moderately and severely impaired.[49]

Recent attempts to stem this general aversion include a variety of publications. The recent two-volume series prepared by the Gerontological Society, *Working with Older People*, is geared to practitioners of various backgrounds with the aim of updating the knowledge base and addressing appropriate services and structures for a continuum of services to the aged. As is pointed out in these materials: "Enough is known about the health trajectories or patterns of health maintenance and decline that preventive steps can be taken in time.... We cannot stress enough the need for practitioners and planners to be aware of individual needs and the available community services in order that timely cross and multiple referrals and actions are provided to people by agencies in cooperation with one another."[50]

The authors of this series also noted: "The heart of what should be assessed is an individual's ability to function as an independent adult, especially with respect to the activities of daily living . . . health or physical disability status, ability to provide for one's psychosocial needs.[51]

That all old people are not alike but represent a range of health and service needs, different racial and ethnic backgrounds, family structures and support systems and structures, socioeconomic backgrounds, current income levels, life experiences and styles, and personalities has been amply demonstrated in the gerontologic literature and is by now a truism. Yet, as is painfully evident, relatively little has been done to recognize and preserve the individualities of the aged, especially the aged in need of long-term care that often involves shifting modalities of treatment.

Even among health-care practitioners specifically interested in the chronic diseases, the rapidity with which conditions among the elderly may shift has often been neglected. The differences in symptomology between younger and older patients, too, is often ignored. A simple, horrible, and not uncommon example is that a toxic confusion may be misdiagnosed as a psychiatric disorder of old age. Accordingly the patient is treated psychiatrically rather than medically. The subtlety of conditions among the aged, too, may be bypassed by family members and practitioners not attuned to the possible numerous variations in the natural history of disease among the old. To date, relatively few health personnel and facilities have met this challenge perhaps because the therapeutic skills required represent a change from the past. Then, too, although demographers had predicted the rise in older population, we have simply been unprepared to develop truly new models of care.

Although a variety of rehabilitative and treatment modalities, including therapeutic milieu,[52] group occupational and social techniques,[53] enrichment of social environment,[54] and individualized treatment of excess disabilities have been used with the institutionalized elderly,[55] the evidence hints that the positive impact of even very carefully designed programs has been of limited scope and duration. That "the best is none too good" poses two awkward but important questions felt keenly by gerontologists, geriatricians, and others involved in treatment of any disabled group of people: What is a successful program? and How much does it cost?

Certainly humanitarian values mandate that attempts to upgrade living conditions and provide effective therapy are to be preferred to passive acceptance of current patterns. Since 1965 federal legislation such as Medicare, Medicaid, and the Older Americans Act has underscored this concern, and gaps in the new service structure as well as in older ones have been the subject of congressional and individual inquiry. Yet the basic reality is that many programs are inappropriately geared to anything other than meeting basic needs for food, shelter, custody, and short (sometimes serendipitous) alleviation of the varieties of disability associated with being old. Perhaps, if we can do no better, this is enough. But a lingering sense of discontent remains.

Why, for example, has so little been done to enable the elderly to remain at home? Perhaps one reason that the coordinated community services required have been slow to develop is that too large a social emphasis has been placed on institutions as solutions to the problems of deviants, including mentally and physically disabled of all ages. There is no reason to think that old people who need help in self-care differ from other old people about their feelings toward institutionalization. For example, a study of protective care projects indicated that the most frequent services requested by the elderly needing help in self-care was for a homemaker, not for institutional care. The United States has lagged behind many other nations in developing home-help services for the aged. When countries are ranked according to the number of home helps per 100,000, the United States falls in group C (2 to 18 per 100,000) along with France, Israel, Japan, and Austria, although our demographic profile is closer to countries in group A—Sweden, Norway, Netherlands, and Great Britain—where there are 100 or more homemakers available per 100,000.[57]

While public intervention on behalf of the aged is considered more appropriate than for other age groups or categories of needy people, the elderly who require care are often still treated as worthy poor whose needs are not quite respectable.[58] Relatively little attention has been paid to the quality of their lives. Many services required by old people do not come to the surface unless the family is ill equipped financially to provide care or where there is no family at all. Social responsibility has been only tangentially extended to ensure both quality and quantity of care for all old people, and it has been easy to avoid the issue of unified and comprehensive community health services. Many people are in institutions not only because of disabilities but because it is profitable to others for them to be there or because no more appropriate facilities in community exist.

Allied to the lack of a range of appropriate community facilities for many elderly is the structure of financing of care. Although this affects the public and the private sector in different ways, there is some suggestion that the present system of private ownership of care-giving facilities such as nursing homes impedes provision of high-quality care and easy transfer of persons from chronic disease hospitals to nursing homes. However, the record of public institutions has been far from perfect. Nor have old people and their relatives been potent lobbyists for change. As poor, needy, infirm, or confused consumers, they have been disadvantaged in demanding service geared to maintaining themselves in the community as long as possible. Federal and state funding has tended to be earmarked for partial or total institutional care or for program planning; limited funds have been appropriated for home help, home nursing, or hot meals.

Furthermore, the patchwork design and financing of existing services makes it difficult for any system to deliver comprehensive care that would enable the impaired elderly to remain at home. There is a need for institutional care. Even with a plethora of community-based services, some proportion of the old will require long-term inpatient care at one time or another. The level of care required will simply be too great and too expensive to be provided at home. Nor can family members cope with the constant need for supervision and support that some elderly people require. The legacy of legislation such as Title III of the Older Americans Act may be to enable appropriate coordinated and integrated services to be delivered to the old at home or in inpatient facilities, where constant attention is given both to the quality of life and care appropriate to the specific needs of the older person.

## Notes

1. Australian Government Social Welfare Commission, *Care of the Aged* (Australian Government Printing House: Tyshwick, A.C.T., 1975), p. 45.

2. Anton Antonovsky, "Social Class Life Expectancy and Overall Mortality," in *Patients, Physicians and Illness*, ed. E. Gartly Jaco (New York: Free Press, 1972), pp. 5-31.

3. Victor Fuchs, *Who Shall Live?* (New York: Basic Books, 1974).

4. Thomas McKeown, R.G. Record, and R.D. Turner, "An Interpretation of the Decline of Mortality in England and Wales During the Twentieth Century," *Population Studies*, 29(1975):391-422; Thomas McKeown, *The Role of Medicine: Dream, Mirage or Nemesis?* (London: The Nuffield Provincial Hospitals Trust, 1976).

5. Zhores A. Medvedev, "Caucasus and Altay Longevity: A Biological or Social Problem?" *The Gerontologist* 14(1974):381-387.

6. Benjamin Franklin, *Some Account of the Pennsylvania Hospital* (Baltimore: Johns Hopkins, 1754).

7. Brigette Berger, *Societies in Change* (New York: Basic Books, 1971).

8. Peter Lazlett, ed., *Household and Family in Past Times* (Cambridge: Cambridge University Press, 1972); Peter Lazlett, *The World We Have Lost* (London: Methuen, 1965); J.D. Chambers, *Population, Economy and Society in Pre-Industrial England* (London: Oxford University Press, 1972).

9. Erving Goffman. *Asylums* (New York: Anchor Books, 1961), pp. 4-6.

10. Ibid., pp. 6-12.

11. Ibid., pp. 6-12.

12. Ibid., pp. 74-92.

13. Ibid., p. 4.

14. Frances Scott, "Factors in the Personal Adjustment of Institutionalized and Non Institutionalized Aged," *American Sociological Review* 20(1955): 538-546.

15. Sheldon Tobin and Morton Lieberman, *The Last Home for the Aged* (San Francisco: Jossey-Bass, 1976).

16. U.S. National Center for Health Statistics, *The National Nursing Home Survey* (Washington, D.C.: Government Printing Office, 1979), table 23.

17. Ibid.

18. Ibid., table 26.

19. Ibid., table 24.

20. Ibid.

21. Ibid., table 25.

22. Ibid.

23. Mary Adelaide Mendelson, *Tender Loving Greed* (New York: Vintage Books, 1975), p. 52.

24. Ibid., p. 187.

25. David Shulman and Ruth Galanter, "Reorganizing the Nursing Home Industry: A Proposal," *Milbank Memorial Quarterly (Health and Society)* 54(1976):132.

26. Peter Townsend, *The Last Refuge* (London: Routledge and Kegan-Paul, 1962); Samuel Levey et al., "An Appraisal of Nursing Home Care," *Journal of Gerontology* 28(1973):222-228; R.H. Holmberg and N.N. Anderson, "Implications of Ownership for Nursing Home Care," *Medical Care* 7(1968):300-307.

27. Mendelson, *Tender Loving Greed*, p. 52.

28. U.S. House of Representatives 95th Congress, Select Committee on Aging, *National Crisis in Adult Care Homes* (Washington, D.C.: Government Printing Office, 1977).

29. Elizabeth Markson, Ada Kwoh, Elaine Cumming, and John H. Cumming, "Alternatives to Psychiatric Hospitalization for Psychiatrically Ill Geriatric Patients," *American Journal of Psychiatry* 124(1971):1055-1062.

30. Shulman and Galanter, "Nursing Home Industry," p. 130.

31. U.S. House of Representatives, *National Crisis.*

32. Werner M. Mendel, "The Case for the Closing of the Hospitals," in *State Mental Hospitals: What Happens When They Close,* eds. Paul I. Ahmed and Stanley C. Plog (New York: Plenum Publishing, 1976), pp. 21-29.

33. Irving Rosow, "Old Age: One Dilemma of an Affluent Society," *The Gerontologist* 2(1962):182-191.

34. Alexander Comfort, "Age Prejudice in America," *Social Policy* 7(1976):4.

35. Barney H. Glaser and Anselm L. Strauss, "The Social Loss of Dying Patients," *American Journal of Nursing* 64(1964):119-121; Elizabeth Markson, "A Hiding Place to Die," *Trans-action/Society* 9(1971):48-54.

36. Karen David, "Equal Treatment and Unequal Benefits: The Medicare Program," *The Milbank Memorial Fund Quarterly (Health and Society)* 53 (1975):449-488.

37. Aaron Wildavsky, "Doing Better and Feeling Worse: The Political Pathology of Health Policy," in *Doing Better and Feeling Worse: Health in the United States*, ed. John H. Knowles (New York: Norton, 1977), p. 110.

38. David Reisman and Donald Horton, "Notes on the Deprived Institution," *Sociology Quarterly* 6(1965):3-20.

39. Elizabeth Markson and Jennifer Hand, "Referral for Death: Low Status of the Aged and Referral for Psychiatric Hospitalization," *International Journal of Aging and Human Development* 3(1970):261-272.

40. Barbara B. Manard, Cary S. Kart, and Dirk W.L. van Gils, *Old Age Institutions* (Lexington, Mass.: Lexington Books, D.C. Heath and Co. 1975).

41. Cary S. Kart and Barbara Beckham, "Black-White Differentials in the Institutionalization of the Elderly," *Social Forces* 54(1976):901-910; Douglas Holmes et al., "The Use of Community Based Services in Long Term Care by Older Minority Persons," *The Gerontologist* 19(1979):389-397.

42. Hobart Jackson, "Planning for the Specially Disadvantaged" in *Alternatives to Institutional Care for Older Americans: Practice and Planning*, ed. Eric Pfeiffer (Durham, N.C.: Center for the Study of Aging and Human Development, 1973).

43. Manard, Kart, and van Gils, *Old Age Institutions.*

44. Ibid.

45. Elizabeth Markson, "Ethnicity as a Factor in the Institutionalization of the Ethnic Elderly," in *Ethnicity and Aging: Theory, Research and Policy,* eds. Donald E. Gelfand and Alfred J. Kutzik (New York: Springer Publishing Co., 1979), p. 34.

46. Lester Thurow, "Not Making It In America: The Economic Progress of Minority Groups," *Social Policy* 6(1976):5-11.

47. Data in this section are taken from U.S. National Center for Health Statistics, The National Nursing Home Health Survey.

48. Institute of Medicine, *Aging and Medical Education* (Washington, D.C.: National Academy of Sciences, 1978).

49. Ibid.

50. *Working With Older People: A Guide to Practice*, vol. II (Rockville, Md.: Department of Health, Education and Welfare, Health Care Financing Administration, Health Standards and Quality Bureau, 1978), p. 5.

51. Ibid.

52. Wilma Donahue et al., "Rehabilitation of Geriatric Patients in County Hospitals: A Preliminary Report," *Geriatrics* 15(1960):263-274.

53. L.Z. Cosin, "Experimental Treatment of Persistent Senile Confusion," *International Journal of Social Psychology* 4(1958):24-42.

54. B.L. Mishara, "Affects of a Rehabilitation Program for Chronic Elderly Mental Patients" (Paper presented at the Seventy-ninth Annual Meeting of the American Psychological Association, 1971).

55. Elaine M. Brody, Morton H. Kleban, M. Powell Lawton, and Miriam Moss, "A Longitudinal Look at Excess Disabilities in the Mentally Impaired Aged," *Journal of Gerontology* 29(1974):79-84.

56. A.D. MacDonald and W.C. Martin, "The Legitimacy of Public Intervention on Behalf of Older Persons: A Three Generation Study," *The Gerontologist* 12(1972):65.

57. Walter Beattie, "Aging and the Social Services," in *Handbook of Aging and the Social Sciences*, eds. Robert Binstock and Ethel Shanas (New York: Van Nostrand Reinhold, 1977).

# 9 Social Welfare Policy and Aging: Implications for the Future—Between The Good Earth and Pie in the Sky

*Robert Morris*

A discussion of social policy and the future is fraught with certain hazards, and it is best to acknowledge this at the start. First, social policy is often confused with a particular program or set of programs. In reality a policy for the aging is a general sense of direction, with many alternative programs capable of realizing that direction. Second, the term *policy* may be circumscribed by one's view of *the social services*, a most ambiguous term. I will consider *social* as meaning any collectively or publicly organized approach to aging in which social agencies or social workers, as we now understand those terms, may or may not play a central role.

The subject of aging falls between two popular approaches. One is idealistic and considers aging as not being old but as a process of becoming. In that approach we should be interested not in security but in autonomy. In that view it is the effort to ensure security for the elderly which threatens their autonomy not the realities of their physical or social conditions. This applies to the younger aged, at least until their powers fail. At the other extreme is the scientific view that medicine, nutrition, and genetic manipulation will extend life and ultimately abolish decrepitude and debility. There is little evidence that such an approach can do little more than defer the onset of debility but that does not reduce the glamour of the approach. The approach in this chapter is to concentrate on the area that lies between these extremes. Any one of us may require the attention of others as we grow older, and this attention may require a publicly supported program of some kind to deal with the human realities of disability.

## Some Background for Aging Policy

Many of the reported facts about wants and requirements of the elderly are widely known, but one set of facts is not well understood. These facts inevitably highlight the relatively improved status programs for the elderly achieved in the past two decades. Socially underwritten conditions for the elderly, whatever their specific deficiencies, have improved greatly compared to a generation

121

ago and in contrast to others in the population. The social position of the elderly
has improved in the following major ways:

1. A minimum income floor is guaranteed with the least oppressive means-
   testing. Although the minimum floor may be inadequate, it is still more
   satisfactory than that provided others and is inflation indexed.
2. The elderly are covered by health insurance, even though its coverage
   is shrinking.
3. With the virtual drying-up of subsidized housing, the elderly are perhaps
   the only sector of society that has built for them any low-cost housing
   regardless of how inadequate that supply is.
4. In the past ten years there has been a significant expansion in home-
   delivered services for the enfeebled elderly.
5. Oppressive limitations on employment in the legal sense, meaning enforced
   retirement at sixty-five, have been substantially relaxed.
6. Finally, a combination of economic-social and medical-technology develop-
   ments have produced a longer life span for more elderly.

All told such programs represent about 24 percent of all federal expenditures and perhaps 8 percent of the gross national product. We can differ about
the exact sum and its significance, but we cannot deny the basic situation.

This recital of achievements must, of course, take note of counterinfluences
such as: the impact of inflation which affects the elderly equally with all others
and even more severely in view of their fixed incomes; the increase in co-insur-
ance and deductibles for health care which leaves the elderly paying out of
pocket about as much for their personal medical care as they did before the
enactment of Medicare; the virtual drying up of a low-cost rental housing supply;
and the increasing loss of mobility coming with increasing age for larger percentages of the population.

After such gains there is a period of substantial confusion in which relative
privilege is offset by continuing pressures—all of which lead to a conflict among
varied special interests, among whom the aged are one, seeking their fair share
of a limited resource pool. This resource pool is even further limited by the
current resistance of the tax-paying citizen.

This resistance shows up in the current resistance to tax rates and regulation
and rule-making by federal and state agencies, which are perceived as government invasion of private lives. Together these two resistances erode public confi-
dence in the capacity of government to deal satisfactorily with social needs.
This resistance is increased by basic social and economic trends. As the proportion of aged in the population increases, technical capacity permits the production of more goods with fewer workers. But these fewer adult workers must
support, through taxes, an increasing proportion of dependents: the aged,
children, and the disabled.

Out of this confusion of trends, about one-third of all human service expenditures are devoted, in one way or another, for the requirements of the elderly. But a general framework for establishing resource distribution in the general interest of society is lacking, and as a result there is still the clash of numerous special interests. In that clash the elderly do not speak with a unified voice. If everyone faces financial constraint, what is the most equitable approach for the elderly?

In this troublesome situation I am almost reluctant to note one positive development for the profession of social work—the evolution of programs of the elderly has created a great opportunity market for social work. Many services and programs for the elderly have grown substantially in recent years, and in some ways the growth of our professional industry is taking place in this arena, not elsewhere. Programs associated with Title XX, Area Offices on Aging, home-health agencies, and training programs all constitute this growth opportunity which may or may not continue. However, this attractive employment situation is not without its negative picture. Social workers, by and large, are employed in agencies and are parts of public or private bureaucracies, and it is in just the influence which such bureaucracies exercise over many of the minutiae of daily existence that complaints about the welfare state arise. This is not unique to the aging, but there is a very strong current of objection to the extent to which public and voluntary agency employees with a mass of regulations and professional procedures intrude on the individual's capacity to control his own life.

## A Few Recurring Issues

A few basic welfare issues are confronted, recede from popular attention, and recur persistently. No widely accepted framework has emerged with which to manage them. They can be summarized thus in oversimplified fashion.

### Control Over One's Own Life

For all persons, but especially for the elderly, continued control over the conditions of one's existence probably constitutes the most powerful of all desires. Assurance of income and good health are the most significant means for retaining control over one's own affairs. This explains the very great bias in public programs in favor of cash payment to individuals. There are two issues regarding cash income for the future that affect what social workers will be doing. One of these derives from the question, How much will the working adult population be prepared to give up in its current income to improve the living conditions for the earlier generation? Whatever income is provided for the elderly today is provided out of the current earnings of the working population. Once this awkward matter is settled, there still remains the question of how income programs will be organized. Will growth be in the direction of equalization in which all elderly are slowly moved to an even level of income, or will public programs continue on behalf of the disadvantaged only. No satisfactory arrangements have been worked out to resolve the choice between equalization and targeting for the disadvantaged mainly because of the intractable character of the notch effect that separates the two. However, for social workers, this leads to a second question.

## What Social Services Will Individuals Pay for?

If the bulk of the programs are devoted to giving control over the life affairs of individuals through adequate income, social workers need to consider what will be offered to the elderly for which they will be willing to pay. That is, what would individuals be willing to purchase directly at a price that would yield enough agency revenue to support professional salaries and status? This is in sharp contrast with the current professional viewpoint which is that services will mostly be paid for by direct grants to agencies to pay salaries, in which circumstance the agency decides what services will be given, and the aged are limited to that which is offered. The answer to this issue may well determine the level of tax-supported programs as well as setting limits to private practice.

## The Future Allocation of Health Resources

Next to income, medical care constitutes the single most important issue continuously raised by the elderly. Without minimizing the importance of the elderly's access to acute medical care when necessary (and this is only reasonably assured today under Medicare), they are still left with the problems of how to continue to live with an assured increase in physical limitation and disability for which medical care offers no relief. What share of the health dollar should be allocated, not to more hospitalization and more visits to the doctor's office, but to the provision of those personal care supports which are essential, if individuals with irreversible and irremediable physical limitations are to continue to live with reasonable control over their own lives and out of institutions? I refer, of course, to the variety of home care, chore, and transportation services that these conditions require. I am not referring to psychological or personal counseling about how to live with disability, but rather what proportion of resources will be allocated to the financing of the concrete social supports that must be made available.

At present the flurry of interest in catastrophic health insurance distracts attention from the issue without solving it. Such insurance will increase payments for high technology health care in hospitals but pay nothing for care outside of a hospital. Since over half of hospital patients have had their condition for over a year, but few patients will stay in a hospital for more than a few days or weeks, the limits of this action can be seen easily.

Social workers have played a minor, not a leading, role in the controversy over this reallocation. Instead there has been a historic tendency to become interested in the periphery of the problem. Social work has been concerned first with counseling and advising rather than with assuring that these social supports are provided concretely. There is also a professional tendency to be attracted by the more exotic and exciting periphery of the health situation. The most striking current example is the rush of social workers to the hospice movement and concern with easing the last stages of dying. Important as this stage is, it inevitably looms less important to the elderly than how they are going to live a large part of their lives with some limitation.

In this situation it is surprising to realize that neither the social-welfare systems nor the social-work professions have sought to create a parallel social support system addressing the aged as the medical system now serves the aged for medical needs only.

*The Rights and Obligations of Family and*
*Support Systems*

The rights and obligations of family members and informal social support systems as compared with the obligations of government and voluntary agencies is another basic issue. Social workers have lived a long time with what has become a cliche—that their services are intended to reinforce family strength. A close examination of the work in reinforcing family life indicates the nature of the future issues with which they must grapple. An estimated 75 to 80 percent of all attention to the needs of the elderly are now provided by family members directly without much assistance from formal agencies. But family capacity is changing for clear reasons. There is no indication that, on average, family willingness to maintain bonds of affection with their elders has declined. What is changed is the absolute situation that the family confronts. General levels of family income and well-being have been improved by the capacity of both husbands and wives to enter the labor force. When an elderly parent requires a substantial amount of physical and personal care, what share of this family well-being should be reduced in order to contribute to the cost of care of the elderly?

More seriously, there has been a loss of the man and woman power conventionally considered to be available to attend to many needs of older persons. Housewives are no longer satisfied to do what is conventionally called "women's work," and they enter the competitive labor market. Unemployed male youths are not easily attracted to jobs, even where they exist, that provide this kind of work. The change in the nature of family composition, with the reduction in the number of children born and serial marriages, all thin out the extensiveness of the family network that once was available to meet the informal needs of many persons.

This trend has fueled much of the programming for the elderly but has left unanswered a central question: What are the shared responsibilities between the family and the formal agency? The rights of families and the elderly have been discussed but not their obligations. When should agency intervention be triggered off, and how shall it be delivered in relation to family's willingness to assume responsibilities themselves. The conventional professional view has been that this can be decided on a case by case basis, assessing each situation. It is important to acknowledge that this places in the hands of the professional person, the social worker, the complete power and authority to decide when and when not to help. This power is at odds with another professional belief in the right of individuals to choose. But if individuals have the right to choose what they will do, they do require some guidance about what society considers it right and appropriate for them to be responsible for also. If supportive services are available to families for the health needs of their aged, one cannot quarrel with family members if they take advantage of those opportunities without asking questions about what they should do before taking advantage of the proferred service. But in a period of limited resources, these services are not a free good. Since rationing of some kind must take place, it is necessary to confront how the level of family obligation will be determined and what circumstances will trigger intervention. Among the ideas that have been advanced in this connection is one that suggests that it is possible to establish not only a ceiling on the maximum amount of help that is available but also a threshold that identifies the minimum social expectation of family responsibility and obligation before social provision is activated.

*Meaningful Use of Time*

In the next decade there will be an older population that is not only older in years but is also substantially better educated than in the past. This issue involved not only the opportunity to be economically employed if desired, but also the opportunity to maintain social contacts and an exchange with other members of society. Social workers will have little control over employment opportunities. The other gratifying uses of time are hardly provided directly by social services, although they can be facilitating in access to leisure activities. The most constructive approach to this issue lies in assuring that those things are done that will permit the elderly to maintain the ties of association which they have developed through their lifetimes and to encounter new and stimulating experience where they desire it. Both of these objectives depend primarily on the maintenance of transportation and mobility. The recreational activities which social welfare can organize are useful but hardly compete with the rich range of social activity that the rest of society provides the elderly if only they have mobility.

There is one area in which the social-work enterprise could make a major contribution to the meaningful use of time; that is, in opening up its own agencies to employment for older persons where they have the physical capacity and the interest. Social-work jobs constitute a major industrial arena for employment. If social workers are serious about the demand that interested elderly should have an opportunity to perform useful and creative tasks, they need to confront their own resistance to the use of older persons in their own agencies in employment of either a part-time or full-time nature. Obviously taking a step of this kind causes difficulties vis-à-vis the professional standards. However, social workers have opened their doors to the baccalaureate worker, and large proportions of the elderly have a baccalaureate degree.

*The Issue of the Quality of Life*

The issue of the quality of life is too complex to develop here, however, social workers can make a contribution in the areas of counseling and advocacy. Many social institutions need a leavening personnel to train others employed in those institutions about the special and distinctive requirements of the elderly, and a certain amount of counseling and social service in agencies will probably be required for a generation or two. If the focus of this social-service function is to be on quality of life, social workers will have to emphasize the normal capacities of the elderly rather than their deficiencies. This includes an emphasis on their capacity to function independently, but more slowly, than a fast-moving youthful generation. Speed in travel, offices, stores, and confusion in computerization that characterize modern life are hardly conducive to well-being in old age.

In one sector—the nursing home, home for the aged, hospitals—the elderly are virtually helpless captives of bureaucracies. Limitations on possessions, movement, choice as to food and clothing demean life. Physician abuse is not uncommon, even if not always intended. Training a constantly changing attendant staff is a weak protection. More useful is the daily presence in such institutions of volunteers who cannot be co-opted nor intimidated by staff routines. Families can serve this function, but most institutional aged have no families or they are far away.

It is in this institutional sector that welfare can most directly affect the quality of life for older persons in a significant way. Although only 5 percent of the aged may live in an institution at any one time, at least one in five or one in four older persons will live in an institution before they die.

Here a profession can do more than it has to understand what changes in the running of these institutions will make it easier for staff to act more decently and humanely. Education is not enough, for the present institutional jobs are nearly unbearable. Perhaps other case mixes in nursing homes will help, or rotation in jobs for staff, use of part-time staff, or more frequent staff relief. More improvements in pay and in staff selection for aides, attendants, and kitchen help will also do more to transform institutional life than marginal increases in professional consultation.

## The Future of Publicly Administered Programs

Perhaps most important of all is the issue of the future of publicly administered programs in America. We have been lulled, by forty-five years of unparalleled growth in the welfare-state idea, into taking public programs for granted, forgetting how and why they came into being. Public hospitals, welfare departments, child-care agencies, and homes for the aged came into being because neither the marketplace nor private social services adequately took care of all people and all conditions, especially not the most disabled or the poorest or the most minority identified persons. In recent years a violent reaction has set in, some justified and some fueled by forces that never accepted a public responsibility. We confront the proper concern of tax-paying citizens that the share of their income taken away by taxes to pay for a stranger's welfare has gone up (as it has risen to pay for military and agricultural and industrial subsidies). At the same time the proliferation of many programs has let loose a flood of regulations and paper demands which confine, bedevil, and restrict all of us. The smallest parts of our lives are now affected and many feel the trend has gone too far. This combination of rising deductions from earned incomes plus the confusions of complex bureaucracies forces many to go back to an earlier period. One such period is the free market. Let individuals buy and pay for what they want. Historically this approach has meant that the poor and those with high-cost needs get little attention. Another path, often taken by social workers, is to try to funnel available tax dollars to private agencies and away from the public ones. This is usually done without any obligation by the private agencies to provide the full coverage for the toughest cases which public agencies must provide.

The issue needs to be confronted squarely soon. If we are to dismantle public programs and rely on tax dollars to feed the market or voluntary efforts, what kinds of obligations will we permit government to impose on the market and on voluntary effort? Or, lacking that, will we be satisfied to let them perform as they will and do nothing about the toughest problems to which we know they cannot, or will not, attend? The current stampede away from government administration toward the proprietary or the nonprofit arena can produce total neglect; wider government controls; or retention of a poor law, second-rate, underfunded system to take care of the leftover problems which the market and the voluntary fields will bypass.

## Some Policy Directions for Social Welfare

The period ahead is not an especially comfortable one as regards a continuance of the present arrangements that social services have fallen into. A better way to blend technical knowledge about aging and human feelings about individuals needs to be considered. If a policy approach for social workers is to be presented at the 1981 White House Conference on Aging, the following suggest themselves as challenging possibilities.

1. Enhancing the elders' control over their own existence is one approach. This is expressed best in the fields of income maintenance and health. If we opt for maximum personal control over one's life, then the position would be that a variety of concrete services that the elderly request, and will pay for, be provided under circumstances largely controlled and determined by the elderly themselves. This would involve increased support for concrete services in health, income, and transportation on a universal basis with the minimum amount of gatekeeping by social workers and others. Instead of case determination, the decisions about when to purchase specific tangible services would be left in the hands of the elderly themselves with economic means at whatever level the United States chooses to afford. A specific example lies in the home care-personal care field. Instead of making these services available only on a clinical assessment basis, the means to purchase personal care within clear limits would be placed in the hands of the elderly through disability allowances. Since rationing would be necessary, more routine rationing devices such as disability indices, income levels, and the like could be introduced.

If, on the other hand, this is an undesirable approach, we can only fall back upon clinical criteria, which means lessening the amount of personal control by the elderly. Organizations would then continue to employ professional personnel, sometimes social workers, sometimes others to do the gatekeeping and decide who is entitled to what service, when. If this approach is opted for, a major challenge would be to devise organizational ways that are less bureaucratic then those that now prevail. Is there any way of maintaining a gatekeeping function in professional hands where staff is accountable for living within limited resources without the flypaper of entangling regulations? At the present time it is estimated in the medical field alone that about 20 percent of all expenditures go for administrative paper work, and in other fields the percentage probably runs much higher. Can this be reduced responsibly? No one has yet produced an answer.

2. Social work's position on the scope of family obligations as well as rights can be crucial. As a profession it could be argued that the whole service system for the elderly be socialized, in which instance a case for more taxation, organization, and bureaucracy would have to be prepared and on grounds that are persuasive.

Alternatively it could be argued that there are some areas of work to be left predominantly in the hands of families when the social-service sector will be activated only after some threshold is crossed. In this kind of mixed, shared system, the technical means whereby the line between rights and obligations is drawn still has to be developed.

3. A reversal of social workers' and citizens' reliance on government solely as a financing faucet for voluntary organizations which cannot be held socially accountable for their work is another possibility. One path is to greatly strengthen government control over private efforts, a path that is inconsistent with tradition. The other is to rescue publicly administered programs from the decay into which they have fallen: to raise public perception of why public programs exist at all, and then to engage in the kind of surgery on public-program administration that will make it once again responsive to citizen's standards. I do not know just what that surgery can be, but we will quickly need to develop better ways of running large public programs with public dollars. This forces attention to employee and public misperceptions about what these programs are about. It affects the nature of labor-management relations. It affects the ethical understanding that citizens are prepared to apply to their society and that means to the organizations they create to underpin that society.

If this could be done, voluntary organizations could be free to do what they do well, and public programs could be supported for what they must do. They could find ways to live together.

4. Another challenge is the quality of life, the meaningful opportunities for the elderly. Social work's major contribution here would be the provision of employment opportunities—part-time or full-time—for the elderly in social-work programs or even slowly relinquishing control over services to the elderly in some manner yet to be devised. Such an approach obviously presents a challenge to the current emphasis on increasing the professional controls over social work practice and employment and the preoccupation with licensure standards.

Alternatively social welfare could develop the position that all the social services (income maintenance, housing, schools, medical care, and the like) require some kind of internal mechanism to sensitize those systems to the distinctive requirements of the elderly, including their changed tempo, the difficulty of intergenerational communication, and so on. Social welfare professions could carve out a primary role in host agencies simply to service other systems in order to sensitize them to these variations for the elderly.

## Where Can Social Work Act Most Effectively?

There are a few focal points where welfare professionals can impact the lives of the elderly more directly. One such area for social work (as distinguished from social-welfare services) lies in administering and staffing certain kinds of specialized services: home-care programs, nursing homes, and residential accommodations.

Social work can also strengthen the case for its functioning in medical-care systems as a host agency. Here it can function either to sensitize the rest of the medical-care system (something not easy to accomplish given the marginal position that social work holds in medicine), or social work can carve out a function important to the medical system which is best carried out or executed by social workers, namely, the humane management of long-term care arrangements for hospitalized patients.

For quality of life and meaningful life opportunity, senior centers and day centers constitute a possible frontier. Mainly these would be utilized not so much for the simple entertainment function that they conventionally provide but rather for the conversion of these activities into opportunities for the elderly to play significant controlling roles in an employed capacity. There are almost endless opportunities for useful civic opportunity. One organization in Boston has been most imaginative in finding gratifying opportunities for the elderly to conduct architectural surveys, staff public-information booths, and so on, but such activities were not developed by social workers. Can social work convert its interests along such lines?

The Area Offices on Aging and the various administrative and planning instruments with which contemporary society is beset, provide an opportunity to employ a few social workers. Can they articulate the case strongly for Area Agencies on Aging to act as a meaningful and planning control mechanism in the evolution of other social programs? If yes and if they can do this in ways that are persuasive in the competition for limited resources, then there will be a national institutional network to sustain attention for the difficult chores that lie ahead.

Finally, at least for the next generation, it is likely that various educational institutions and agencies will still require specialized training in the needs of the elderly, which education can be provided in part by social workers. But this will be effective only if social work concentrates on improving its understanding of the wants of the elderly rather than on any narrowly defined concept of what social work itself is about.

# Epilogue

Unfortunately there are no all-inclusive answers or pat recommendations with which to conclude that provide policy directions most advantageous or appropriate for the aged population today or in the foreseeable future. The authors herein have delineated a variety of areas to which public policy should be addressed, demarked problems and barriers to optimal aging in contemporary society, and suggested a variety of approaches—both concrete political changes and more subtle attitudinal and behavioral issues which may enhance or inhibit development of flexible yet substantive social policies. Just as no general agreement exists about the specifics of "a good old age," there is no consensus about ways in which this state may be achieved. Yet there is an increasing concern with the prerequisites for each individual to achieve a good old age according to his or her own definition. These include obvious and fundamental needs: for a decent income postretirement, a comfortable home, activities appropriately geared to the interests and health level of people, learning opportunities, friendship and social support networks, and provision of newly designed, as well as tried and true, modalities of health and social service delivery. Perhaps the most crucial question one may ask in evaluating directions in social policy for the aged is, "Would I want to live in a society such as is being proposed?" And equally important, "Would such a society be both economically viable and permit all elderly of disparate backgrounds and interests to live with dignity?"

# Index

# Index

# About the Contributors

**Stanley M. Grabowski** is professor of education and chairperson, Division of Continuing Education and Special Programs, School of Education, Boston University. Dr. Grabowski offers "Teaching Older Adults" in the Boston University Summer Institute in Gerontology. He edited, with W. Dean Mason, *Learning for Aging*, published by the Adult Education Association, and he has written several training texts in gerontology, including (with Gretchen Batra) *Technique of Teaching: A Programmed Instruction Text for In-Service Educators in Long-Term Care Facilities*, published by the National Technical Information Service. He is a member of the Executive Committee of the Boston University Gerontology Center.

**Beth B. Hess** is professor of sociology at County College of Morris (N.J.) and visiting associate professor, City University of New York Graduate Center. A Fellow of the Gerontological Society, she has written articles published in *Society, Research on Aging, Social Policy, The Family Coordinator,* and *SIGNS*. Her edited reader, *Growing Old in America* (Trans-Action 1976), is now in its second edition, and an introductory textbook, with Elizabeth W. Markson, *Aging and Old Age* (1980), has just been published by Macmillan, Inc. Professor Hess's three areas of interest—friendship, aging, and feminism—converge in her chapter for this collection.

**Ruth H. Jacobs** received the doctorate from Brandeis University at age forty-five after a career as a journalist. She is a professor of sociology at Boston University, where she teaches gerontology courses to undergraduates and, in the Summer Institute, the course "Aging and Alternative Life Styles" to graduate students and clinicians. She has published two books, *Life After Youth: Female, Forty, What Next?* (Beacon Press) and, with Barbara Vinick, *Re-engagement in Later Life: Re-employment and Re-marriage* (Greylock Press). Dr. Jacobs is currently engaged in research on displaced homemakers.

**Louis Lowy** is professor of social work and associate dean, Boston University School of Social Work, and also a member of the Department of Sociology and the Graduate School of Arts and Sciences faculty, Boston University. Cofounder of the Boston University Gerontology Center, Dr. Lowy's extensive activities in the field of aging currently include: member of editorial boards, *Journal of Gerontological Social Work, Aging and Human Development,* and *International Journal of Psychosocial Gerontology*; cofounder and president, American-Swiss Committee of Social Work; Fellow of the Gerontological Society, and member, House of Delegates, Council on Social Work Education. Books published in 1979 include *The Challenge and Promise of Later*

*Years: Social Work with the Aging* (Harper and Row) and *Kooperation freitatiger und beruflicher Mitarbeiter in Sozialer Diensteer.*

**Allan R. Meyers**, an anthropologist with training in sociology, history, demography, and public health, is assistant professor in the Department of Socio-Medical Sciences at Boston University School of Medicine and adjunct assistant professor of anthropology at Boston University's College of Liberal Arts/ Graduate School. Dr. Meyer's main research interests concern the use of health and social services, the interface between formal and informal networks, and the use and abuse of alcohol by older adults. He is also concerned with the establishment of better communications among research, education, and service-delivery personnel.

**Robert Morris** is emeritus professor, former Kirstein Professor of Social Planning, and director of the Levinson Policy Institute, Brandeis University. The author of numerous articles and books on planning, social service, organization, medical care, and aging in professional and scientific journals, Dr. Morris has been active in the public-policy arena as a planning consultant and administrator for various agencies, including the U.S. Veterans Administration, U.N.R.A.A., and the Council of Jewish Federations and Welfare Funds. He has served as member or chair of the American Foundation for the Blind, National Institute of Mental Health, and the Conference Board of Associated Retired Persons. Dr. Morris is a past president of the Gerontological Society and a fellow of the American Public Health Association.

**Gary Orgel** combines backgrounds in law and philosophy in his positions as assistant professor of philosophy, Department of Philosophy, and director, Philosophy and Medicine Program, Boston University. His areas of specialization include philosophy of medicine, philosophy of law, social and political philosophy, and phenomenology and existentialism. In the area of gerontology, he recently taught the course "Conflicts and Commitment: Ethical Issues in the Care of the Elderly" at Boston University.

**Elliott Sclar** is associate professor of urban planning and chair of the Division of Urban Planning at Columbia University. An economist who specializes in economic development and health and human-service planning, Dr. Sclar is presently directing a major study of economic change and mental health-service utilization in Fitchburg, Massachusetts. He has taught a course on the politics and economics of aging at the Boston University Summer Institute in Gerontology since 1976. He was formerly on the faculty of Brandeis University and chief of economic research and health planning at the Veterans Administration's Geriatric Research, Educational and Clinical Center at the Boston Outpatient Clinic. He has written a variety of books and articles exploring the themes of economic development and individual well-being and of aging.

# About the Editors

**Elizabeth W. Markson** is associate research professor of sociology at Boston University and research coordinator, Boston University Gerontology Center. A member of the board of directors, Society for the Study of Social Problems, and past president of the Massachusetts Sociological Association, she has written articles which have appeared in *Trans-Action/Society, Journal of Gerontology, The Gerontologist, American Journal of Psychiatry,* and *SIGNS. Trends in Mental Health Evaluation,* edited with David Franklyn Allen, was published by Lexington Books, D.C. Heath and Co., in 1976. An introductory gerontology text, *Aging and Old Age,* with Beth B. Hess, was recently published by Macmillan. Dr. Markson's areas of interest include medical sociology and social psychiatry, aging, and women's issues.

**Gretchen R. Batra** holds the positions of director, Summer Institute in Gerontology, and planner/coordinator: education at the Boston University Gerontology Center. As director of the Summer Institute, Ms. Batra has worked with the contributors to this book, all of whom have been faculty in the Institute or lecturers in the Institute's Distinguished Lecture Series. In addition, she develops, implements, and evaluates conferences and workshops cosponsored by the Gerontology Center and various schools and departments at Boston University, as well as local and national organizations and agencies. She coauthored, with Stanley Grabowski, *Technique of Teaching: A Programmed Instruction Text for In-Service Educators in Long-Term Care Facilities,* published in 1978 by the National Technical Information Service.